ARMY SACRIFICES

>─┤◆├─◦─┤◆├─<

Briefs from Official Pigeon-holes

>─┤◆├─◦─┤◆├─<

JAMES B. FRY

With a new introduction by Jerome A. Greene

STACKPOLE
BOOKS

0 11557 02824 9

New introduction copyright © 2003 by Stackpole Books

Published by
STACKPOLE BOOKS
5067 Ritter Road
Mechanicsburg, PA 17055
www.stackpolebooks.com

All rights reserved, including the right to reproduce this book or portions thereof in any form or by any means, electronic or mechanical, including photocopying, recording, or by any information storage and retrieval system, without permission in writing from the publisher. All inquiries should be addressed to Stackpole Books, 5067 Ritter Road, Mechanicsburg, Pennsylvania 17055.

Cover design by Tracy Patterson

Cover photo courtesy of the United States Military History Institute, Carlisle, Pennsylvania

Printed in the United States of America

10 9 8 7 6 5 4 3 2 1

FIRST EDITION

Library of Congress Cataloging-in-Publication Data

Fry, James B. (James Barnet), 1827–1894.
    Army sacrifices : briefs from official pigeon-holes / by James B. Fry ; with a new introduction by Jerome A. Greene.—1st ed.; [Stackpole Books ed.]
        p. cm.—(Frontier classics)
    Originally published: Army sacrifices, or, Briefs from official pigeon-holes. New York : D. Van Nostrand, 1879. With new intro.
    Includes bibliographical references.
    ISBN 0-8117-2824-2
    1. Indians of North America—West (U.S.)—Wars. 2. Dakota Indians—Wars, 1876.
3. Beecher Island, Battle of, Colo., 1868. 4. Fetterman Fight, Wyo., 1866.
5. United States. Army. Dept. of the Missouri. I. Title. II. Series.

E83.866.F94 2003
973.8'1—dc21

                                                                        2003042451

INTRODUCTION

by Jerome A. Greene

When Col. James B. Fry's *Army Sacrifices; or, Briefs from Official Pigeon-Holes* was published in 1879, most of the events described therein were within memory of many of its readers. The book's contents offered a curious mix of some relatively obscure army incidents, together with accounts of significant frontier Indian clashes which had variously garnered public attention between the 1850s and 1870s. It was, as it remains, a miscellany reflective of its time—a post–Civil War portrait of personal deeds and command operations of U.S. Army troops, most of them occurring in the American West during times of purported peace. Its purpose was to honor the so-called peacetime army, and to impart knowledge "of the dangers and privations to which our soldiers in active service in the Indian country are continually exposed." Fry claimed to have based his work on "official reports," and, although this is not always evident within, it is apparent that in his working capacity with the Adjutant General's Department he had access to official records relating to most of the topics of his interest. As such, Fry's book offers a contemporary view of a number of notable episodes that have since attracted the attention of modern historians.[1]

At the time that *Army Sacrifices* appeared, Indian warfare in the West was an ongoing reality, and the book provided as much a reflective look at some of the earlier contests as well as those that more nearly resembled current events. In 1879, tribes in the trans-Mississippi West faced the brunt of white civilian and military pressure to relieve them of their lands and force them onto reservations. The Great Sioux War of 1876–77, with its classic encounters of the Rosebud and the Little Big Horn, was scarcely sixteen months old. The Nez Perce War had occupied almost five months in 1877, and the following year's conflict with the Bannocks and Paiutes was running its course. American Indian policy was on trial in the press. The tabloids had recently reported on the Northern Cheyennes' flight through Kansas and Nebraska from incarceration in the Indian Territory, and in January 1879, they broadcast the bloody escape of many of those tribesmen from imprisonment at Fort Robinson, Nebraska. As Fry's book reached the market, the Utes of Colorado were resisting their agent preparatory to a full-scale outbreak. Yet looming down the years were unforeseen clashes with Apaches in the Southwest, coupled with further troubles among the Sioux that would culminate in the 1890 army massacre at Wounded Knee, South Dakota, a bloody climax to the panoply of Indian-white relations in the West.

Fry's own service in Indian country was limited to three brief tours of duty: service in Washington Territory and Oregon in 1849–50; assignment to Fort Brown, Texas, in 1851–52; and "frontier duty" at Fort Leavenworth, Kansas, in 1860–61. Despite that, he was an avid student of military policy and warfare history, and he knew personally many of the figures who participated in the events he described in *Army Sacrifices*. Moreover, as a military bureaucrat at the highest offices he had access to reports and documents of appropriate authority, with the result that his knowledge of the military side of the events of which he wrote was unsurpassed for his time. He was outspoken, too, and on numerous occasions could not help but interject his opinion and personality into widely diverse military and political controversies of the day.

In poise, temperament, training, and experience, James Barnet Fry personified the consummate professional military administrative officer. Born on February 22, 1827, in Carrollton, Illinois, Fry entered West Point in 1843 at age sixteen and graduated four years later with an appointment of brevet second lieutenant in the 3rd Artillery. He taught artillery tactics at the Military Academy before joining Gen. Winfield Scott's forces at Mexico City as a second lieutenant of a light battery of the 1st Artillery, during the closing months of the War with Mexico. His service there was brief, and Fry was shortly posted to Fort Columbus, in New York Harbor, before being transferred to the Northwest. He embarked by sea, rounding Cape Horn and traveling via Honolulu to gain his station at Fort Vancouver, Washington Territory, in early 1849. (His relatively uneventful passage around South America to the Northwest Coast comprises a chapter in the book.) Fry served briefly at Astoria, Oregon, before returning east to successive post assignments between 1851 and 1853 at East Pascagoula, Mississippi; New Orleans Barracks; and Fort Brown, Texas, along the Rio Grande. In the meantime, he had been promoted first lieutenant on February 22, 1851, his twenty-fourth birthday.

In December, 1853, Lieutenant Fry returned to West Point as assistant instructor of artillery, serving in that capacity until August 1, 1854, when the superintendent, Col. Robert E. Lee, appointed him Adjutant of the

Military Academy, a position he occupied for more than five years, during which he cultivated his flare for administration. In 1859, he joined the garrison of the Artillery School for Practice at Fort Monroe, Virginia, leaving the post to participate in the army campaign to quell John Brown's raid of the arsenal at Harpers Ferry. While at Fort Monroe, Fry served as recorder to a board revising the West Point curriculum, then departed in 1860 for sequential stations with his regiment in Baton Rouge, Louisiana, and Fort Leavenworth, Kansas. By early 1861, he was back in the East, commanding a battery of light artillery at the nation's capital. In appearance, Fry presented a lean yet dignified military bearing, straight-backed and mustachioed, with medium-length hair and a broad forehead and with a strong, thoughtful countenance.

When the Civil War erupted in 1861, Fry's organizational propensities inordinately qualified him for staff assignments, and the balance of his career remained in this area of military service-either in the field or in the office. In March, he became assistant adjutant general, with the rank of brevet captain, in the office of the Adjutant General in Washington, D.C. Two months later, he became chief of staff to Brig. Gen. Irvin McDowell, who commanded the Department of Northeastern Virginia, responsible for defending the nation's capital, and served throughout the campaign leading to First Manassas, July 21, 1861. Appointed captain, Fry became chief of staff to Maj. Gen. Don Carlos Buell, commanding the Department of the Ohio, and received temporary promotion to colonel as additional aide-de-camp to that officer. He later won permanent appointment as major in the position. His assignment to Buell, 1861–62, brought Fry into combat conditions as he accompanied the Army of the Ohio to Tennessee and the Battle of Shiloh, and to Mississippi and the Siege of Corinth. He followed Buell into Alabama and later Kentucky, taking part in the Battle of Perryville on October 8, 1862, and joined the pursuit of Confederate general Braxton Bragg across southeastern Kentucky. Fry won commendations for his performances at Shiloh and Perryville. (However, Fry's expressed belief that Buell had contributed significantly to the outcome at Shiloh won tacit disapproval from Gens. Ulysses S. Grant and William T. Sherman and, despite Grant's endorsement of his appointment to head the Provost Marshal General's Office, may later have benignly harmed his career.)

In November 1862, Major Fry returned to Washington as assistant adjutant general directing the Appointment Branch of the Adjutant General's Office. Promotion to lieutenant colonel shortly followed, and the position evolved into Fry's selection in March, 1863, as the first Provost Marshal General of the United States, with rank of colonel, charged with managing the organization and enforcement of military conscription for the war effort. Besides matters related to desertion, he oversaw enlistment procedures, state quotas, bounties, and measures affecting implementation of the draft, especially in Boston and New York, where rioting had previously occurred. It was a critical position, and Fry performed it masterfully—he was "a cool, determined, fearless organizer, with the highest order of intellectual force." By his own estimation, Fry's work facilitated the induction of more than one million men into the Union Army and the apprehension of more than 76,000 deserters, for which in April 1864 he gained the star of a brigadier general.

Politically, however, Fry's purportedly bad conduct of the office of Provost Marshal General (a view never shared by the War Department, which, conversely, solidly supported Fry's performance), and the issue of its extension when the war ended, evolved into a dispute between Sens. James G. Blaine (Rep.-Maine) and Roscoe G. Conkling (Rep.-New York). Conkling disliked Fry for perceived slights when he, Conkling, had been a prosecutor in New York State during the war, and publicly and exaggeratedly besmirched Fry's administration of the office, which, admittedly, had been plagued in some quarters by corruption and greed. Blaine, who disliked Conkling, sided with Fry in the squabble that occupied the floor of the Senate in April 1866, reading a letter prepared by Fry in his own defense. Conkling's forces ruled the day, however, and Blaine and Fry were worsted in an overt display of partisan politics. When the office was indeed abolished in August 1866, Fry reverted to his former rank of lieutenant colonel. Despite the congressional acrimony over his operation of the bureau, and despite substantial political opposition growing out of the controversy, he received brevet promotions of colonel for "gallant and meritorious services" at Bull Run; of brigadier general, U.S. Army, for his performances at Shiloh and Perryville; and of major general, U.S. Army, for "faithful, meritorious, and distinguished services" during his tenure in the Provost Marshal General's office.[2]

Following the reorganization of the Army after the end of the Civil War, Fry spent the balance of his career at various geographical division headquarters around the country. Late in 1866 he joined the Division of the Pacific (embracing the Military Departments of California, the Columbia, and—after March 1868—Alaska) in San Francisco as its adjutant general, remaining there until May 1869. Reassigned to the same position at headquarters of the newly created Division of the South (encompassing, variously, the Departments of the Cumberland, Louisiana, Texas, and the South), he spent two years in Louisville, Kentucky, during the height of Reconstruction. In July 1871, at the personal request of Lt. Gen. Philip H.

Sheridan, the Army reassigned Fry to the Chicago headquarters of the Division of the Missouri—the largest military jurisdiction in the nation (containing the Departments of the Missouri, the Platte, Dakota, and Texas)—where he performed the duties of adjutant general until November 1873. It was in the vast territory embraced within the division's boundary that many of the events later described by Fry in *Army Sacrifices* took place. Subsequently, Fry transferred to the staff of the Division of the Atlantic (later designated the Department of the East), headquartered at New York City and composing the eastern and Great Lakes states, besides parts of Tennessee and Kentucky. In 1875, he won promotion to colonel. In New York, his health grew bad, and, on surgeon's recommendation in the spring of 1877, he applied for duty with an exploring expedition in the West. Briefly transferred to the Department of the Missouri, Fry for unknown reasons never took the field and returned to New York within weeks.

Over the next three years, Fry's constitution worsened. In November 1878, he was diagnosed with dyspepsia (chronic indigestion), and in the following year went on extended sick leave. His surgeon told him that he experienced "Hyperemia of the membranes of the Brain, induced by long and continued mental labor," as well as glaucoma that was permanently destroying his vision. Ordered to duty in the Division of the South in December 1879, he protested that "New Orleans would probably finish me."[3] Colonel Fry thus remained at the New York City offices until his retirement from the Army on July 1, 1881, on his application, after thirty-four years of continuous service. *The Army and Navy Journal* extolled him as a "patriot, scholar, soldier, and gentleman" and "a man of the highest culture, kind and benevolent, a true adherent of the golden rule." Fry remained in New York City for several years before moving to Newport, Rhode Island, where he died from a brain aneurysm on July 11, 1894, at age sixty-seven. He was laid to rest in the churchyard of St. James the Less, in Philadelphia, Pennsylvania. Fittingly, the Adjutant General of the U.S. Army represented the War Department at his interment.[4]

During the last several years of Fry's divisional assignments, he began producing the tomes that marked him as a respected soldier-historian. Following his retirement, he spent his remaining years carrying on his literary projects, producing a spate of articles, monographs, and books about army procedures and military history. Besides *Army Sacrifices*, Fry's notable publications include *Final Report of the Operations of the Provost-Marshal-General in 1863–66* (Washington, D.C., 1866); *A Sketch of the Adjutant-General's Department of the United States Army from 1775 to 1875* (New York, 1875); *The History and Legal Effect of Brevets in the Armies of Great Britain and the United States* (New York, 1877); *McDowell and Tyler in the*

Campaign of Bull Run, 1861 (New York, 1884); *Operations of the Army under Buell* (New York, 1884); and *Military Miscellanies* (New York, 1889). Fry also contributed articles and book reviews to the *Army and Navy Journal*, *The Century* (including its prominent "Battles and Leaders of the Civil War" series), *North American Review*, and *Journal of the Military Service Institution of the United States*. Late in life he offered a subdued perspective of the political mêlée surrounding the Conkling-Blaine dispute, entitled *The Conkling and Blaine-Fry Controversy, in 1866* (New York, 1893). This volume seems to have afforded Fry solace from the wounding impact of the rancorous matter that had affected him so personally.[5]

Fry likely researched and wrote most of *Army Sacrifices* while serving in the Division of the Missouri under Sheridan, because many of the pertinent descriptive records of the events depicted therein would have been housed in its Chicago offices. Certainly, he accessed documents in the Washington offices of the War Department, as well as army-sanctioned tabloids like the *Army and Navy Journal*, to facilitate his work. With the exception of Fry's fairly detailed treatments of the Modoc War in California, 1872–73 (the longest piece), the Wagon-Box Fight, 1867, and a few other essays, particulars of the events as given are often sketchy. Sources are usually not identified, and inflated description (such as that of the Cheyenne, Roman Nose, on pages 22–23) is a hallmark. The first names of individuals introduced in the text are often excluded, and dates are often ignored. Brevet rank is confusingly employed with reference to individuals. Nor did Fry always provide sufficient context about his topics, while his prose assumed a stilted Victorian flavor (notwithstanding a flair for the dramatic) that reads awkwardly today. Occasionally, he (or his editor) erred in the spelling of Indian tribal names and place names ("Pah Vaut" and "Eutaws" for "Paiute" and "Utes," respectfully, on page 49; "Mounted Knee Creek" should be "Wounded Knee Creek" on page 120). And inexplicably, the chapters are presented in no chronological order according to subject. Nor, quite frankly, are all of his chosen subjects reflective of the book's title. Throughout, the terminology and attitude regarding Indians as "savages" of low intelligence is generally reflective of the attitude of the period in which Fry wrote.[6]

When Fry produced *Army Sacrifices*, the full context of the Indian wars was not yet available to him, although the final outcome seemed inevitable. There was no question that the nation's martial forces would emerge supreme in the longstanding contest between civilization and savagery, and the theme is manifest throughout Fry's writing. And while he sympathized with the Indians' plight, he embraced widely pervasive Darwinian notions of the racial superiority of whites that foresaw the physical decline of the tribes. His answer to the "Indian problem" simplistically recommended that native people "establish habits of obedience to regulations," a militaristic and unrealistic solution that spoke volumes of his ignorance of the subject. The Indian, he wrote, should be absorbed by civilian communities and "enabled and required to hold fast where located while the frontier passes beyond them." Fry did, however, foresee an innovative attempt at integration—the experimental enlistment of Indians into the army that occurred between 1891 and 1897.[7] In fairness, Fry's meager knowledge of Indians typified that of those army officers who spent most of their careers on staff duty in eastern offices far removed from the scenes of action.

The fourteen chapters presented a potpourri of frontier events, some unfamiliar to modern readers that seemingly border on folklore and were probably not drawn from "official pigeon-holes." Some, like the Fetterman affair, the Beecher Island fight, and Capt. Guy V. Henry's winter march read in 1879 like recent history pulled from the headlines of the day. One, "The Penitentes," described the intriguing religious sect of Catholic and native origin centered in 1870s New Mexico Territory that was (and remains) prone to superstition, "barbarous rites," and suffering. Another, "Bill and Dan," presented the adventures of brothers drawn west by opportunity, but whose reward for their tenacious perseverance was murder by scoundrels. Despite its peripheral topics, the substance of *Army Sacrifices* lay in its period narration of Indian wars battles. The volume affords an important contemporary look at episodes of the Indian wars by one close to the scene during an age when the conflicts were front-page news. Readers contemplating Fry's assessments might do well to consult modern studies of those campaigns and engagements.[8]

Oddly, although the defeat and death of Lt. Col. George A. Custer and his 7th cavalrymen at the Little Big Horn had but recently captured the nation's attention, and would certainly have qualified as an "army sacrifice," Fry failed to capitalize on its public appeal and spoke but tangentially of the events of the Great Sioux War of 1876–77 in *Army Sacrifices*. But it was not because he had nothing to say on the subject. Indeed, within a month of the catastrophe, Fry published in the *Army and Navy Journal* (July 22, 1876) an essay explaining his view of the basis for the army loss. It was a well-reasoned and clearly stated analysis of the causes for Custer's defeat according to the record at the time. It included Fry's judgments regarding Brig. Gen. Alfred H. Terry's orders to Custer that were—and have since been—a catalyst for dissent among those with more than a passing interest in the Battle of the Little Big Horn. In his essay, Fry, among other things, took the view that Custer was well within the scope of Terry's instructions in acting as he did; his argument remains persuasive more than a century after its appearance. In 1889, Fry included the paper in a compilation of his writings, *Military Miscellanies*.[9] (Because of the continuing interest in Custer and the Little Big Horn, and because the nature of the topic otherwise paralleled the contents of *Army Sacrifices*, Fry's 1876 essay, as presented in his *Military Miscellanies*, is herewith included in this reprint.)

Fry's 1876/1889 commentary about Custer and the Little Big Horn was not his last statement on the subject. Early in 1892, he weighed in again, elaborating on his previous remarks in observations published in *The Century* to accompany an article entitled "Custer's Last Battle," by Capt. Edward S. Godfrey, who had fought under Maj. Marcus A. Reno at the Little Big Horn. Fry's "comments" rearticulated in further detail his earlier stance on the matter of Custer's adherence to Terry's orders, once more concluding that that officer's movements were appropriate and within tolerance for the conditions he found before him. Moreover, they suggested that Terry perhaps acted in his own self interest in his official reports of the tragedy, and that "the utter failure of our campaign was due to [the government's] underestimating the numbers and prowess of the enemy."[10] Not all military men agreed with Fry, however. Nearly four years later, Col. Robert P. Hughes took him to task in the pages of the army's elite professional periodical, *The Journal of the Military Service Institution of the United States*. Hughes was the brother-in-law of the then-dead Terry, whose memory, Hughes believed, had been sullied by Fry's comments imputing (as interpreted by Hughes) that the failure of the campaign largely rested with Terry. Of course, by the time Hughes's article appeared in January 1896, Fry himself was dead. The debate over whether Custer disobeyed Terry's orders, however, continues to this day.[11]

Fry's predilection for injecting his opinion into matters of controversy, especially during the years following his retirement, gave him a reputation in army circles as something of an intellectual gadfly. His arguments in Custer's defense inflamed the passions of those who disliked Custer and some made clear their feelings toward Fry in their private correspondence. Maj. James S. Brisbin, who had served in the Sioux-Cheyenne campaigns of 1876–77, distained Fry's remarks, telling an associate that "there has been nothing since the birth of Christ that old Fry does not think he knows all about." Much of the bias reflected the invisible schism that existed between West Point graduates and non-graduates. Retired Maj. Frederick W. Benteen, a Little Big Horn veteran referencing the Godfrey-Fry items in *The Century*, stated that "Gen. Fry and Godfrey have the mystic characters 'M.A.' [Military Academy] after their names in the Army Register, and . . . those fellows think that no one had a right to know anything quite as well as they do." Later, Benteen described Fry as "a finicky, cynical, . . . d——d fool, with an unlimited amount of brass, and little else, though he thought he was an author, genius and all'round [sic] grand man."[12] In fact, the assessment said more about Benteen, a contentious officer who spent his final years slandering those who had been more successful than himself.

Army Sacrifices received mixed reviews. Military commentators praised it to their readers, the *Army and Navy Journal* even tendering prepublication notice. "Our regular army of the present day having no historian," stated the *Journal*, "these sketches . . . serve a useful purpose and furnish ample material for the 'collaborateur' of the future." Its contents depicted "the hardships and sufferings endured by our soldiers [on the Indian frontier] . . . of which the world knows nothing," a statement not altogether true considering the then-ongoing press coverage of the Indian wars. The *Journal* extolled Fry for rendering "a most excellent service to the Army in offering this contribution to the history of its trials and achievements."[13] *The Nation's* review was more critical, reproaching him for "slipshod" writing as well as for a "want of comprehensive and historic knowledge" in setting forth his ideas on solution of the Indian question.[14] It was surely a proper complaint at a time when indigenous people were increasingly attracting scientific interest and when viewpoints about them were changing. Indeed, it is this very dichotomy of a bygone era that makes *Army Sacrifices* a measure of its time and place, a volume worthy of the present reprinting. In this respect, the book resonates a compelling view of frontier Indian conflicts for readers yet allured by their study and interpretation.

NOTES

1. Following its 1879 publication, Fry's book reappeared in 1887. The 1887 edition bore on its cover and spine the imprint, *Indian Fights— Illustrated—1887*, although the title page retained *Army Sacrifices*. In the later version, the order of the table of contents and the preface was reversed. The 1887 edition also contained pen and ink illustrations by Frederic Remington and engraved portraits by other artists that were not included in the initial printing.

2. For particulars of the dispute with Conkling and the subsequent airing on the floor of the Senate, see Donald Barr Chidsey, *The Gentleman from New York: A Life of Roscoe Conkling* (New Haven: Yale University Press, 1935), 81–92. See also, *Congressional Globe* (39th Cong., 1st sess.), Part I, 2–151, 2293 (including Fry's letter); and Part V, 3935. Fry's account of the events, published in 1893, is referenced in the text below.

3. Matters addressing Fry's health, including pertinent quotes, are from James B. Fry, Appointment, Personal, and Commission File, 2910 ACP 187 in National Archives, Record Group 94, Records of the Office of the Adjutant General (National Archives Microfilm Publication M1395) (hereafter referred to as Fry, ACP). See also, Jack D. Welsh, *Medical Histories of Union Generals* (Kent, Ohio: Kent State University Press, 1996), 120–21.

4. Sources for Fry's career consist of his Appointment, Personal, and Commission File, 2910 ACP 187 in National Archives, Record Group 94, Records of the Office of the Adjutant General (National Archives Microfilm Publication M1395); George W. Cullum, *Biographical Register of the Officers and Graduates of the U.S. Military Academy at West Point, N.Y., from Its Establishment, in 1802, to 1890* (3 vols; Boston and New York: Houghton, Mifflin and Company, 1891), II, 314–15; *The Association of the Graduates of the United States Military Academy, Annual Reunion, June 10th, 1895* (Newburgh, NY, 1895), 15–23 (including first quote); Circular No. 12, November 1, 1894, Military Order of the Loyal Legion of the United States; William H. Powell (comp.), *Powell's Records of Living Officers of the United States Army* (Philadelphia: L. R. Hamersly and Company, 1890), 224–25 (containing information provided directly from Fry); Francis B. Heitman (comp.), *Historical Register and Dictionary of the United States Army, from Its Organization, September 29, 1789, to March 2, 1903* (2 vols.; Washington, D.C.: Government Printing Office, 1903); *Army and Navy Journal*, July 9, 1881; *Army and Navy Journal*, July 23, 1881; *Harper's Encyclopedia of United States History, from 458 A.D. to 1902* (10 vols.; New York and London: Harper and Brothers Publishers, 1902), III, 484–85; Ezra J. Warner, *Generals in Blue: Lives of the Union Commanders* (Baton Rouge and London: Louisiana State University Press, 1964), 162–63; *Webster's American Military Biographies* (Springfield, Mass.: G. and C. Merriam Company, Publishers, 1978), 131; and *Who Was Who in America* (Chicago: A. N. Marquis Company, 1967), Historical Volume, 262. Information regarding post–Civil War divisional offices to which Fry was assigned appears in Raphael P. Thian (comp.), *Notes Illustrating the Military Geography of the United States, 1813–1880* (Washington, D.C.: Government Printing Office, 1881), *passim*.

5. A relatively complete listing of Fry's works appears in *The Centennial of the United States Military Academy at West Point, New York* (2 vols.; Washington, D.C.: Government Printing Office, 1904), II, 246.

6. See, for example, the discussion in Sherry L. Smith, *The View from Officers' Row: Army Perceptions of Western Indians* (Tucson: University of Arizona Press, 1990), 20–27.

7. On the matter of enlistment of Indians, see, Jack D. Foner, *The United States Soldier Between Two Wars: Army Life and Reforms, 1865–1898* (New York: Humanities Press, 1970), 129–31; and Edward M. Coffman, *The Old Army: A Portrait of the American Army in Peacetime, 1784–1898* (New York: Oxford University Press, 1986), 259–60.

8. For example, in the order of Fry's presentation, for Beecher Island, see, John H. Monnett, *The Battle of Beecher Island and the Indian War of 1867–1869* (Niwot, Colo.: University Press of Colorado, 1992); for the Fetterman fight, see, Dee Brown, *Fort Phil Kearny: An American Saga* (New York: G. P. Putnam's Sons, 1962); for Henry's march, see, Thomas R. Buecker, "'The Men Behaved Splendidly': Guy V. Henry's Famous Cavalry Rides," *Nebraska History*, 78 (Summer, 1997), 54–63; for the Wagon Box Fight, see, Jerry Keenan, *The Wagon Box Fight: An Episode of Red Cloud's War* (Conshohocken, Penn.: Savas Publishing Company, 2000); for the Grattan affair, see, Lloyd E. McCann, "The Grattan Massacre," *Nebraska History*, 37 (March, 1954), 1–25; and for the Modoc War, see, Erwin N. Thompson, *Modoc War: Its Military History and Topography* (Sacramento: Argus Books, 1971). For the Penitentes, see Alberto Lipez Pulido, *The Sacred World of the Penitentes* (Washington, D.C.: Smithsonian Institution Press, 2000).

9. "Custer's Defeat by Sitting Bull," in Fry, *Military Miscellanies* (New York: Brentano's, 1889), 506–11. Fry's original essay appeared without attribution in the *Army and Navy Journal* , July 22, 1876, 804–5, under the title, "A Glance at the Recent Disaster."

10. Edward S. Godfrey, "Custer's Last Battle, By One of His Troop Commanders," *The Century Illustrated Monthly Magazine*, 43 (January, 1892), 358–84. The piece was immediately followed with "Comments by General Fry on the Custer Battle," 385–87 (quote is on 385). The Godfrey-Fry pieces are available to modern readers in William A. Graham (comp., ed.), *The Custer Myth: A Sourcebook of Custeriana* (Harrisburg, Penn.: The Stackpole Company, 1953), 125–55; E. S. Godfrey, *An Account of Custer's Last Campaign and the Battle of the Little Big Horn* (Palo Alto, Calif.: Lewis Osborne, 1968) (with an introduction by Robert M. Utley); and E. S. Godfrey, *Custer's Last Battle, 1876* (Olympic Valley, Calif.: Outbooks, 1976).

11. Hughes's article, "The Campaign Against the Sioux in 1876," *Journal of the Military Service Institution of the United States*, 18 (January, 1896), 1–44, appears in reprint appended to William A. Graham, *Story of the Little Big Horn* (Harrisburg, Penn.: Military Service Publishing Company, 1952). For later discussion of the controversy surrounding Custer and Terry, at least partly spawned by Fry, see, Cyrus Townsend Brady, *Indian Fights and Fighters* (New York: Doubleday, Page, and Company, 1904), 359–97; Charles Kuhlman, *Did Custer Disobey Orders at the Battle of the Little Big Horn?* (Harrisburg, Penn.: The Stackpole Company, 1957) (especially as relating to Hughes's discussion of events); Francis B. Taunton, *"Sufficient Reason?" An Examination of Terry's Celebrated Order to Custer* (London: English Westerners' Society, 1977); and Tom O'Neil and Hoyt S. Vandenberg, "A Modern Look at Custer's Orders," *Research Review: The Journal of the Little Big Horn Associates*, 8 (June, 1994), 10–20.

12. Brisbin's remark is quoted in Utley's introduction to Godfrey, *An Account of Custer's Last Campaign and the Battle of the Little Big Horn*, 11. Benteen's remarks appear in Benteen to Theodore Goldin, January 11, 1896; and Benteen to Goldin, February 22, 1896, in John M. Carroll (comp.), *The Benteen-Goldin Letters on Custer and His Last Battle* (New York: Liveright, 1974), 238, 279.

13. *Army and Navy Journal*, February 8, 1879 (first quote); *Army and Navy Journal*, February 22, 1879 (second and third quotes).

14. *The Nation*, May 1, 1879, 305.

CUSTER'S DEFEAT BY SITTING BULL[1]

by James B. Fry

Speaking broadly, battles, as public events, are always sharp and conspicuous. Their results are immediate and important. These are reasons why we are both hasty and extravagant in criticizing the parts played in them by the principal actors. Before we have sufficient information to deal modestly with praise or blame, we commence an arbitrary and lavish distribution of glory and shame. The erection of monuments to the dead, and the sinking of bottomless pits for some of the living, are begun before the smoke has sufficiently cleared away to permit a fair view of the battlefield; and it often happens that information which should have been patiently waited for, comes in time to stop both the monument and the pit, before the one has risen above, or the other sunk below, the surface of the earth.

As will be seen further on, it is not our purpose to discourage the noble sentiment that is manifesting itself in subscriptions for a monument to Custer. We aim only to enjoin moderation in judgment and action towards all concerned in the recent disaster on the Little Big Horn. There are two sides to every case, but in this instance one side is silenced by death. General Terry has been placed in a somewhat false position by the relative order in which his two reports reached the public. The second one, marked "Confidential," and evidently intended only as an explanation to his military superior, Sheridan, was, accidentally, the first received, and was evidently published in response to the public anxiety; whereas the official report of the occurrence was not received at Army Headquarters, and could not be given out, until an erroneous impression, to the effect that Terry had been eager to seize the public ear in his own defence—had been created by the confidential explanation. These two reports taken in connection with such other reliable information as has come to hand, justify certain general references:

1st. The enemy was underrated by Sherman, Sheridan, Terry, Crook, and Custer. It should be borne in mind that when Custer left Terry, June 22, both were ignorant of the fact that the enemy they were seeking had defeated Crook on the 17th of that month.

2d. Ignorant of the enemy's real strength and prowess, Terry, as well as Custer, thought that the 7th Cavalry (12 companies) under the latter officer, was fully able to defeat the Indians, the only trouble apprehended being to catch them. This is shown by the fact that Custer did not want, nor did Terry require him to take, the Gatling battery, which would have retarded his movements, but strengthened his command, and the fact is admitted in Terry's confidential explanation, where he says, "he expressed the utmost confidence that he had all the force he could need, and I shared his confidence." Under this impression Terry, the commander, being fully and solely responsible for the strength, equipment, and orders of Custer's force, started that officer on the expedition. That Custer thought he was strong enough does not relieve Terry of his responsibility on that point.

3d. As to the instructions from Terry under which Custer moved. They are dated June 22. Reno had just returned from a scout in which he had discovered the Indian trail, but had turned back without pursuing it to contact with the Indians. Terry says to Custer—having furnished him with fifteen days' rations—"You will proceed up the Rosebud *in pursuit* of the Indians whose trail was discovered by Major Reno a few days since. It is impossible to do so, the Department Commander places too much confidence in your zeal, *energy* and ability to wish to impose upon you precise orders which might hamper your action *when nearly in contact with the enemy.*" The Department Commander, in general terms indicated his "views," but did not require compliance with, if Custer saw a sufficient reason for a departure from, them. There was evidently no material difference of understanding between the two officers. In Terry's confidential explanation of July 2 to Sheridan, as well as in his letter of instructions of June 22 to Custer, the point of prime importance was to get Custer to the south of the enemy, and this because Terry feared the Indians would escape if they had the least opportunity to do so. It was not in Terry's instructions, and it clearly was not in his mind that Custer, if he came "in contact with the enemy," should defer fighting him until the infantry came up.

We knew but little of the country except that it was wild, very broken, and without roads. It was surmised that the enemy was on the Little Big Horn River, but his position was, in point of fact, unknown. He was known, however, to be vigilant, to move with celerity, and to possess a thorough knowledge of the country. There could be no justification for any plan of operations which made an attack dependent upon a junction between Custer and Gibbon, after three or four days' march from different points, in the wilderness.

The views which Terry expressed as to Custer's best line of march would probably have carried the latter farther to his left—the south—than he went. But these were views to be acted upon or disregarded at Custer's discretion, and they were evidently expressed with no eye to Custer's danger, but solely to prevent the dreaded escape of the enemy.

Admitting for the moment that Custer had gone quite to the south of the enemy, and that Gibbon was known to be approaching from the north, there were, still, wide doors open for escape. This was not an enemy to be leisurely bagged, and if Custer had simply watched him, as soon as the Indian vigilance showed Gibbon to be in dangerous proximity, he would have escaped, and Custer would have suffered disgrace for not attacking with a force the sufficiency of which had been admitted by all concerned. Without further argument the inference is fair that, finding himself in the presence of the enemy whose flight was to be expected, with its well known serious consequences to our side, and having no knowledge of Gibbon's position, Custer was right in attacking.

4th. For the marches to the fatal field, the preliminaries to the attack, and for the plan of battle, Custer was clearly responsible. Terry says that Custer told him he would march at the rate of about thirty miles a day, but adds that "on the 22d he marched twelve miles, on the 23d, twenty-five miles, from 5 A.M. until 8 P.M. of the 24th, forty-five miles, and then, after night, ten miles further, resting but without unsaddling, and then twenty-three miles to the battlefield," the implication being that some blame attached to Custer for not conforming more nearly to the thirty miles average. It is easy to understand that through a very difficult and unknown country, no great regularity could be expected in the marches of a large military force. Water and grass must be reached at due times, unforeseen obstacles have to be overcome.

It has been asserted that, smarting under the wounds which preceding events had inflicted upon his pride, Custer dashed recklessly into this affair for the purpose of eclipsing his superior officers in the same field, regardless of cost or consequences. This is going too far. Custer was doubtless glad of the opportunity to fight the battle alone, and was stimulated by the anticipation of a victory which, illuminating his already brilliant career, would make him outshine those put on duty over him in that campaign. But his management of the affair was probably about what it would have been under the same circumstances, if he had had no grievance. His mistake was in acting in mingled ignorance of, and contempt for, his enemy. He regarded attack and victory in this instance as synonymous terms, the only point being to prevent the escape of the foe. Under this fatal delusion he opened the engagement, with his command divided into four parts, with no certainty of cooperation or support between any two of them. Three companies, under Benteen, were far away on the left, ordered in, it

xviii   CUSTER'S DEFEAT BY SITTING BULL.

is true, and by chance they arrived in time to aid Reno. Once company, under MacDougal, was in the rear with the pack train. Reno was sent to the left bank of the river to attack the enemy with three companies, while Custer with the other five companies not only remained on the opposite bank from Reno, but moved back of the bluff, and three miles lower down the stream, thus placing mutual support, in case of necessity, out of the question, and fell into a complete or partial ambuscade.

Neither ambition, nor wounded vanity, prompted these fatal dispositions, nor were they due to lack of knowledge of the principles of his profession. They proceeded, as heretofore stated, from a misconception, which Custer shared with others, in relation to the numbers, prowess, and sagacity of the enemy.

NOTES

1. "Custer's Defeat by Sitting Bull," in Fry, *Military Miscellanies* (New York: Brentano's, 1889), 506–11. Fry's original essay appeared without attribution in the *Army and Navy Journal*, July 22, 1876, 804–5, under the title, "A Glance at the Recent Disaster."

PREFACE.

OUR regular wars, campaigns, and battles have secured their places in history, and fame has been distributed, and in some cases redistributed, among the actors in these great events. It may be said, without any spirit of criticism, that the people, thankful for the manifest and immediate advantages which they receive through great victories, are generous in bestowing honors for them. Rewards for these services are graded more by the magnitude of the general results than by the individual heroism displayed. Furthermore, the field for personal prowess in grand operations, where the results are obtained through the aggregated efforts of large numbers, is small compared with that afforded by encounters which put the courage, skill, and endurance of a trusty few to the

1

severest test. The so-called peace life of our army officers is made up largely of adventures of the latter kind. For these services the regular army of the United States has no historian. The record of its deeds of heroism and self-denial, of its labors and sacrifices in the cause of civilization and of progress, lies buried in the dusty pigeon-holes of the Government. Occasionally a book appears giving the history of a regiment or the biographical sketch of some eminent commander, but of the real services and trials of the army at large but little is known to the public. Now and then some deed of more than ordinary heroism or some Indian massacre of unusual atrocity is chronicled in the daily press, and read as news, but is allowed to pass without appreciation or reward. This is the inexorable decree of fate. Time and discrimination are indispensable to the proper classification of public services, and the regular army must patiently and confidently await the verdict, which cannot be much hastened.

The following brief sketches of actual occurrences, scattered over a period of nearly thirty years, are presented as examples of the

dangers and privations to which our soldiers in
active service in the Indian country are continually exposed, and the gallantry and fortitude they display. The recitals are mainly
recasts of official reports, in some instances
without a change even in the terms. They
have been elaborated, however, by confir-
matory information of a reliable character.
The archives of the Government abound in
reports of encounters and sufferings of which
those presented in this little volume are merely
illustrative cases selected from memory. A
thorough examination would disclose, in brief
and unpretending papers, proofs of gallantry
and devotion to duty, by officers and enlisted
men now unknown to fame, which, if set forth
in a true light by able pens, would arouse the
admiration and gratitude of the nation.

It is thought some of the incidents related in
the following pages will be admitted as evidence
of nobler and stronger traits of character than
great battles and grand operations usually produce. Two or three of the sketches, though not
exactly in keeping with the others, are never-
theless true stories, and are inserted to break
the sad monotony of so many accounts of suffer-

ing and death. That the recitals in these pages
exhibit the worst features of the Indian character
is unavoidable, though such is not the purpose
of the work. Driven continually behind our rapidly advancing frontier, plundered and abused
by the more powerful and aggressive race, without one particle of redress for any wrong done him
by the white man, and knowing no law but that
of retaliation and vengeance, it is not strange
that the barbarian should indulge in bloody
deeds. Nor is he afforded an opportunity to
show the provocation for his wrong-doing.
Nearly forty years ago Stone, in his "Life of
Brant"—Thayendanegea—said : "The Indians
are no sculptors. No monuments of their own
art commend to future ages the events of the
past. No Indian pen traces the history of
their tribes and nations, or records the deeds
of their warriors and chiefs—their prowess and
their wrongs. Their spoilers have been their
historians ; and, although a reluctant assent has
been awarded to some of the nobler traits of
their nature, yet, without yielding a due allow-
ance for the peculiarities of their situation,
the Indian character has been presented with
singular uniformity as being cold, cruel, mo-

rose, and revengeful, unrelieved by any of those daring traits and characteristics, those lights and shadows, which are admitted in respect to other people no less wild and uncivilized than they.

"Without pausing to reflect that, even when most cruel, they have been practising the trade of war—always dreadful—as much in conformity to their own usages and laws as have their more civilized antagonists, the white historian has drawn them with the characteristics of demons. Forgetting that the second of the Hebrew monarchs did not scruple to saw his prisoners with saws, and harrow them with harrows of iron ; forgetful, likewise, of the scenes at Smithfield under the direction of our own British ancestors, the historians of the poor untutored Indians, almost with one accord, have denounced them as monsters, *sui generis*, of unparalleled and unapproachable barbarity ; as though the summary tomahawk were worse than the iron tortures of the harrow, and the torch of the Mohawk hotter than the faggots of Queen Mary.

"Nor does it seem to have occurred to the 'pale-faced' writers that the identical cruelties,

the records and descriptions of which enter so
largely into the composition of the earlier volumes of American history, were *not* barbarities
in the estimation of those who practised them.
The scalp-lock was an emblem of chivalry.
Every warrior in shaving his head for battle
was careful to leave the lock of defiance on his
crown, as for the bravado, ' Take it if you can.'
The stake and the torture were identified with
their rude notions of the power of endurance.
They were inflicted upon captives of their own
race as well as upon the whites; and with their
own braves these trials were courted, to enable
the sufferer to exhibit the courage and fortitude
with which they could be borne—the proud
scorn with which all the pain that a foe might
inflict could be endured.

" The annals of man probably do not attest
a more kindly reception of intruding foreigners
than was given to the Pilgrims landing at Ply-
mouth by the faithful Massasoit and the tribes
under his jurisdiction. Nor did the forest kings
take up arms until they but too clearly saw that
either their visitors or themselves must be driven
from the soil which was their own, the fee of
which was derived from the Great Spirit. And

the nation is yet to be discovered that will not fight for their homes, the graves of their fathers, and their family altars. Cruel they were in the prosecution of their contests, but it would require the aggregate of a large number of predatory incursions and isolated burnings to balance the awful scene of conflagration and blood which at once extinguished the power of Sassacus and the brave and indomitable Narragansetts over whom he reigned. No! until it is forgotten that by some Christians in infant Massachusetts it was held to be right to kill Indians as the agents and familiars of Azazel; until the early records of even tolerant Connecticut, which disclose the fact that the Indians were seized by the Puritans, transported to the British West Indies, and sold as slaves, are lost; until the Amazon and La Plata shall have washed away the bloody history of the Spanish-American conquest; and until the fact that Cortez stretched the unhappy Guatemozin naked upon a bed of burning coals is proved to be a fiction, let not the American Indian be pronounced the most cruel of men."

This is a powerful plea for the savage, too strong, perhaps, in some particulars. It must

be admitted, however, that many of his vices
have been learned from us, and the bad faith
and injustice shown in our dealings with the
race have driven it in self-defence to like prac-
tices.   But too much is claimed by the friends
of the Indians in behalf of their original or in-
herent rights.

The acknowledgment that wild tribes are independent sovereignties under the law of nature
or of nations has been the principal source of
evil both to the savage and the nation in dealing
with the Indian question.   They have no form
of government, no conception of justice, no
knowledge of any law except that of retaliation,
and no organization except a rude one for war.
Yet we have treated these wild subjects, living
within the limits of our domain, constituting
part of our population, as independent sove-
reigns, with nominal governments of their own,
and have made and formally ratified treaties with
them.   The main effect of these treaties has
been to confirm and foster the evil which we
should no longer tolerate.   Of course these
treaties have been, and always will be, broken.
It is impossible for either of the contracting
parties to enforce observance of them.   What

chief can keep his followers on a reservation, and what administration can keep white men off it ? And why keep them off ?

If the savages are to be civilized by the whites, the more intimate the contact the better for that purpose. When it is contended that in the interest of Indian improvement *bad* whites should be kept away from his reservation by force, how is it to be decided which whites will be bad as civilizers ? The treaties, based upon prevailing notions, are not only fragile, but their violation, which is inevitable, is almost certain to produce immediate war. Should we not, then, forestall these causes of bloodshed ? The important step in settling the question is to bring the Indian at once under *some* form of government prescribed by the United States, which is now held responsible for his behavior, and in which government he shall be protected and his individual responsibility shall be enforced. To let him live on under the law of retaliation until a few powerless agents and volunteer philanthropists can Christianize him is to make his case a very protracted, if not a hopeless, one. He should be prepared in the most effectual and expeditious way for

absorption by civilized communities. To this
end, instead of driving the savages continually
beyond the frontier and trying to isolate and
herd them together in large bodies, they should,
as far as practicable, be localized in small numbers near the settlements, and enabled and required to hold fast where located while the
frontier passes beyond them.

But the question remains, *how* shall they be
governed now ? Some of them have adopted a
few of the ways of civilization, and, from necessity, have substituted for their own our me-
thods of gaining a livelihood, but they are not
civilized. With nearly if not all of them a vast
improvement must be made by a rigid, personal accountability, in all the elements of
which their society is composed, before they will
be fit to take a part even in self-government.
The wild Indian must be taught to restrain his
propensities so far at least as to conform to
some of our plain and fixed rules of action.
Coercion and not moral suasion is necessary as
the immediate agency in reaching this end.
Rigidity and impartiality in the enforcement of
a few rules, even though they appear harsh, will
do more for the wild Indian's present improve-

ment than a higher and more elaborate code only
feebly executed ; * the important consideration
being to establish habits of obedience to regulations based on the rule of individual rights.
Administration of the first principles of justice among the Indians in their dealings with
each other, as well as with white men, is a duty
we owe to ourselves as well as to them.

To enforce the necessary rules and restraints
requires the constant presence and frequent and
systematic use of force. But the civil authority
is as inapplicable and insufficient for the control
of wild Indian tribes as it is for the suppression
of disorderly whites when banded together in in-
surrection and rebellion. The civil code could
not, without dangerous innovations and prece-
dents, be altered so as to apply to this special
class, even were the civil power strong enough
to enforce it. Military force, and military or
martial law, are probably the only means adequate to meet the requirements, until the condition of this *unconstructed* people will justify
the substitution of the civil for the military
administration of their affairs.

* In this connection see that excellent work " The Indian Question," by Lieut.-Colonel E. S. Otis, U. S. Army.

The conclusions, then, are :

First. Localize the Indians, subdividing tribes into bands, so as to have not more than ten or twelve hundred together, and secure the title of land to them in common by a deed of trust. Let it be good agricultural land—about one hundred and sixty acres to each man—near the settlements, and as far as possible from the opportunity or temptation to hunt. Use all the force necessary to establish the Indians on the locations selected, and to keep them there. Enlist and otherwise employ as many Indians as practicable in the military service.

Second. Place the locations, excepting, of course, all of those where civil law is now in ᐟoperation or can soon be effectually enforced, under martial law, with such special regulations as Congress may prescribe. Administer this law upon white men and Indians alike, within the prescribed reservation, substituting criminal and civil for martial law as rapidly as circumstances in each case will justify.

Third. Permit, subject to the foregoing restrictions, all proper intercourse, especially intermarriage, between the whites and Indians. White men who select Indian wives may be useful instruments in the effort to teach the Indians our customs and mode of life. The locations being kept as near as possible to the limits of civilization, the process of absorption, aided by surroundings, will be the more rapid ; the aim being to teach obedience to the elementary principles of our moral and legal code, rather than to enforce our religion or civilization upon a race which after years of trial has given no positive assurance of ever fully receiving them.

TABLE OF CONTENTS.

SACRIFICES;

OR,

BRIEFS FROM OFFICIAL PIGEON-HOLES.

"The Island of Death."

THE pressure on the Government during the War of the Rebellion deprived the Indian frontier of military protection which it much needed and had previously received. The Indians, fully recognizing the advantages which our internal struggle gave them, became aggressive, exacting, and insulting. They depredated on the settlers, stopped and robbed the overland stages, seized stock, took possession of station-houses, and,

17

when hungry passengers were seated at their meals, turned them out and consumed themselves all of the scanty supply of provisions, and sometimes added murder to their other offences. Seeing the weakness of our military posts, they insulted and taunted their garrisons, and occasionally robbed them also. But, notwithstanding this condition of things on the frontier, the importance of connecting the Atlantic and Pacific by rail, enhanced by the Rebellion, was not lost sight of. Encouraged by the inflation of the currency and its free circulation, and backed by the spirit of enterprise and daring which the war brought into the highest activity, the Union and Kansas Pacific Railroads were pushed out into the Indian hunting-grounds. This was a serious matter for the savages. Major-General Hancock says, in an official report made in 1867: "The extension of our great lines of travel across the plains is driving away the buffalo, and thus interfering with the hunting-grounds of the Indians, and with their

only means of support.   The Government
makes no sufficient arrangements to sub-
sist them where the game has disappeared,
and they are obliged to roam over the
country after the buffalo to support themselves."

With the game driven from his hunting-
grounds by the opening and constant use
of our lines of travel, forbidden by us to
roam at large in pursuit of it, required to
live upon certain reservations of land, with
no other means of subsistence than those
afforded by the Government, and those
wholly insufficient, and with strong convictions as to his rights and his ability to
defend them, the Indian was not likely to
be quiet.

In the winter of 1866 the situation was
alarming to the settlers, and was rendered
more critical by the divided responsibility
of the Indian Bureau and the War Department.   Military commanders were only
able by the most judicious management to
secure from the Indians partial observance
of the flimsy treaties in force.   Satanta,

a Kiowa chief, told Major Douglas, commanding Fort Dodge, that the Sioux were coming down to make a coalition against us in the spring, and that they intended to make war. The Cheyennes, who fiercely opposed the construction of the railways, sought a council with General Palmer, commanding at Fort Ellsworth, Kansas, where the railroad now crosses the Smoky Hill River. Preparations were at once made for the reception of these barbaric lords, with their wild retainers. Two hospital tents were pitched, one for the council and the other to serve as quarters for the guests. A couple of fat steers were slaughtered, and coffee, sugar, and bread in profusion were provided ; for these dusky diplomats never talk on an empty stomach if they can avoid it. They arrived at the appointed time—"Roman Nose," a great war-leader; "Black Kettle," principal chief, and "Big Head," a noted young brave—accompanied by their favorite wives and a few young bucks. When the envoys had rested a day, and

gorged themselves with fresh beef, the officers of the garrison, in full dress, assembled with the chiefs at the council-cham-
ber. After the customary handshaking
the whites arranged themselves across one
end of the tent, facing the reds, who completed the rectangle. For some minutes
there was a quiet but diligent puffing at
a single stone pipe, or calumet, which was
passed around from mouth to mouth, with
a covert wipe of the stem from each pale-
face as it came to his turn. The General
welcomed the Indians in a few well-chosen
words, and asked the object of their visit.
Black Kettle, a fine-looking man of middle
age and heavy features and frame, arose.
He possessed great influence with his
tribe, and by his wise counsel had more
than once averted war. His dress was
simple, with the exception of a massive
necklace of crescent-shaped silver plates,
from the front of which depended a heavy
silver medal bearing the profile in relief
of Washington. It had been presented
long ago by the President of the United

States to one of Black Kettle's * ancestors,
and was worn with evident pride. This
chief spoke at length and to the point.
It was the old story of honest, oppressed
Indians and treacherous, tyrannical white
men.   Much truth was told with native
eloquence, and the Great Father was asked to stop the building of the iron road,
which would soon drive away the buffalo
and leave his children without food.   After
the hearty grunt of approval by his followers had subsided, Roman Nose moved in
a solemn and majestic manner to the centre
of the chamber.   He was one of the finest
specimens of the untamed savage.   It
would be difficult to exaggerate in describ-
ing his superb physique.   A veritable man
of war, the shock of battle and scenes of
carnage and cruelty were as the breath of
his nostrils ; about thirty years of age,
standing six feet three inches high, he
towered giant-like above his companions.

---

* Black Kettle had narrowly escaped with his life at the Chevington
massacre in 1864, and was killed in the attack by Custer on his village
on the Washita, November, 1868.

A grand head with strongly-marked features, lighted by a pair of fierce black
eyes ; a large mouth with thin lips,
through which gleamed rows of strong
white teeth ; a Roman nose with dilated
nostrils like those of a thoroughbred
horse, first attracted attention, while a
broad chest, with symmetrical limbs on
which the muscles under the bronze of his
skin stood out like twisted wire, were some
of the points of this splendid animal. Clad
in buckskin leggings and moccasins elabo-
rately embroidered with beads and fea-
thers, with a single eagle feather in his
scalp-lock, and with that rarest of robes,
a *white* buffalo, beautifully tanned and
soft as cashmere, thrown over his naked
shoulders, he stood forth, the war chief of
the Cheyennes. As he warmed with his
topic his great chest heaved and fire flashed from his eyes. His speech was brief,
as became a soldier, and to the same effect
as Black Kettle's. Unlike the latter, however, he said that never before had he
taken the hand of the white man in friend-

ship, but that he could be a strong friend
as well as a bitter foe, and it was for the
white chief and the Great Father to decide
which part he should play in future.   As
the sequel will show, this was probably the
last as well as the first time he and the
whites joined hands in friendship.   General Palmer assured the speakers that their
words should be faithfully reported at
Washington, but made them no promises.
The delegation left the garrison loaded
with presents, Roman Nose receiving,
among other things, a crimson sash, which
he frequently wore in the bloody battles
that followed hard upon the heels of the
council.

Our war in the interior had now ended,
and our troops were quite ready to turn
their attention to the frontier.   Accordingly, Major-General Hancock moved out
in March, 1867, with a force consisting of
some fifteen hundred men, composed of infantry, cavalry, and artillery, with instructions from General Sherman not to hold
the Indians to account for some murders

which had been the subject of complaint,
but "to make among the Cheyennes,
Arapahoes, Kiowas, Apaches, and Comanches a display of force; to notify
them that if they wished for war they
could have it; and to explain to them
fully that hereafter they must keep
off the routes of travel — railroads and
other roads; that all depredations and
molestation of travellers must cease forth-
with, and that all threatening of our military posts by them, verbally or by message, or otherwise, must cease at once, or
war would ensue." The Indians were neither prepared nor disposed to accept this
challenge as suddenly and formally as it
was offered. They evidently construed the
movement as meaning immediate or pro-
spective war; and, to gain time, they used
diplomacy with skill worthy of a Beacons-
field or a Schouvaloff. Councils and talks
without number and without much sincerity or significance were held.

The state of affairs in the spring of 1867
is shown by General Hancock's official

report of May 14, in which he says : "It
is my present intention to maintain active
operations during the summer, and as late
into the winter as practicable (unless peace
be made meanwhile), against all Sioux and
Cheyennes (save friendly bands of the
former) who may be found between the
Arkansas and the Platte."

The instances of fortitude and bravery
which occurred during the bloody struggle
which now set in are almost "as numerous as grains of sand on the yellow
shore." One engagement furnished an
exhibition of courage, skill, and endurance
unsurpassed, perhaps unequalled, in any
age or clime. General Hancock had been
called to other duty, and General Sheridan
had succeeded him, being accompanied by
Brevet-Colonel George A. Forsyth, major
Ninth United States Cavalry, as acting in-
spector-general. This officer, chafed by
the restraint and inactivity of his staff position, begged of his chief a command in
the field ; but at that period, close on the
heels of the great war and the army reduc-

tion which followed it, leaders were more abundant than followers, and all of the rank and file which could be brought into the field were under command of Sully, Custer, and other able and distinguished officers, and no opportunity for the assignment of Colonel Forsyth, according to his rank, presented itself. But as additional forces were much needed, he was told that, if quite willing to do so, he might raise and lead a force of fifty men, not to be enlisted but *hired* for the occasion at the rate of thirty-five dollars per month, each to bring his own horse and equipments, receiving forty-five cents per day for the use thereof, but to be supplied with arms, ammunition, and rations by the Government. The offer was promptly accepted and the men soon found in the immediate vicinity of Fort Hays. Several of them were ex-soldiers who, having served out their enlistments long before, had adopted the life of the frontiersman, thus making the best possible cross for the purpose in hand. The rest were the ordinary run of their

kind, with two exceptions, the first being
that of an American far above the average
stature, and who appeared pre-eminent in
knowledge of the Indians, of the country,
in daring—in short, in all the qualities
which constitute leadership upon such occasions.   In the confidence he inspired he
was a second Roderick Dhu.   The other
seemed to be inferior, and in all respects
unfit for the service: a Jew, small, with
narrow shoulders, sunken chest, quiet
manner, and piping voice, but little
knowledge of firearms or horsemanship;
he was, indeed, unpromising as a son of
Mars, and, after forty-nine had been obtained, was accepted only in order that he
might be counted on the rolls to make up
fifty and enable the expedition to start.
Lieutenant Frederick H. Beecher, Third
United States Infantry, at his urgent solici-
tation, was assigned as second in command.   He was one of the marvellous pro-
ducts of our civil war.   Active, intelligent,
and distinguished during that long contest, when he came out of it he had lost

the use of one leg, yet insisted upon serving on the active instead of the retired list.
The embodiment of energy and bravery,
rest and fear were words without meaning
to him. A noted guide and good rifle-
shot was *dubbed* acting lieutenant, and
one of the men, being a doctor, acted as
surgeon for the party.

Thus organized—each man, including
officers, armed with a Spencer carbine and
a revolver, and supplied with one hundred and twenty rounds of ammunition, part carried on four pack-mules,
and seven days' rations (consisting
principally of bread and salt) in each
man's haversack—the command took the
field. After scouting for some days a message was received at Fort Wallace from
the Governor of Colorado, saying that the
settlers between Bison Basin and Harbin-
ger Lake were hard pressed by an overwhelming force of Indians, and begging
that Colonel Forsyth would march
promptly to their defence. No orders
or formalities were waited for. The

command turned at once in the direction indicated. Other depredations by the same Indians were soon discovered, and their trail was struck and rapidly followed. It led to the headwaters of Beaver Creek and thence up the Arickaree fork of the Republican River. The repeated efforts of the Indians to mislead their pursuers by dispersing in various directions from time to time were unsuccessful, and on the 14th of September, 1867, the large, fresh trail of a reassembled force was struck and pursued hotly until the afternoon of the 16th. At that time, although not an Indian had been seen, the observant and experienced followers knew that a fight must inevitably take place next day. As the command had no pro visions left except biscuit for one day, and no time to hunt for game, it was desirable to bring on and end the combat at the earliest possible moment. Instead, however, of marching as usual until night, the commander, finding a good grazing spot, resolved to go into camp about five o'clock that afternoon, to give his animals rest and grass and get fully prepared for the events of the morrow. It was well he halted. The Indians had a cunning ambuscade laid for him near by, thinking he would march until dusk and fall into it just at the end of a hard day's journey. The bivouac was established on the bank of the Arickaree, in which stream there was but a few inches of running water. The surrounding country was an open but undulating plain, with hills and ridges a mile or two away, and a few scrubby wild-plum trees here and there in the low places. A sand island in the middle of the stream, directly behind the bivouac, was fringed with willows and bore a few stunted trees. The horses were carefully picketed, a guard posted, and the men lay down near their horses, with their arms in their hands. The commander was up before daylight and on the lookout while others yet slept. Peering steadfastly into the surrounding gloom, he saw, before there was hardly a tinge of light, the

stealthy movement of the approaching
foe.   He instantly called to his men to
hold on to their horses and prepare for
attack.   The call was not a moment too
soon.   The Indians rushed in, shaking
buffalo robes and blankets, yelling and
whooping, for the purpose of stampeding
and running off the animals.   This was
the first move in their plan of attack.   It
failed, and a few rounds drove them back.
But as day dawned their overwhelming
numbers and their preparations for a
general advance became visible.   Colonel
Forsyth instantly decided to take position on the sand island behind him.   It
was oval in shape, some forty feet wide
and two hundred feet long, and was
separated from the mainland by a mere
thread of water.   The well-directed fire
of three chosen marksmen posted in
the grass on the bank kept the Indian skirmishers at bay while the movement of men and animals to the island was
effected.   The animals were tied securely
to bushes, and the men were distributed in

a circle and ordered at once to lie down,
and as soon as possible dig rifle-pits for
themselves in the sand.   The only in-
trenching tools were pocket-knives and
hands ; but the fire of the enemy hastened
the work, and in a few minutes the only
man in sight was the commander, who still
walked erect from point to point, instruct-
ing and encouraging the men.   He went
under cover only when one of the men,
having completed his own shelter, prepared a pit for his chief.   An annoying but
desultory fire was kept up by the Indians
until about nine o'clock, when preparations for a grand assault became visible.
Large numbers of dismounted warriors,
armed with Spencer, Sharp, or Henry rifles (as all of the braves were), and many
boys with bows and arrows, were seen
crawling through the grass and getting
their position in easy range of the island.
Further away on the open plain the
mounted storming party formed for the
charge.   The dismounted men opened a
terrific fire upon the island and the boys

clouded the air with arrows. The plan of
the foe was promptly and fully compre-
hended by Colonel Forsyth. Galling and
destructive as the fire from the grass was, he
would not permit his men to answer it, but
held every gun in readiness to open, at the
word, upon the charging party, which he
knew would soon rush on to ride over and
slaughter them. The fire slackened; women and children lining the hills, just out
of range, began their unearthly yells and
wild dances, and three hundred mounted
warriors, painted and stripped, with the
"dog-soldiers"—the desperadoes from various tribes—in front, all led by a grand
chief whose waist was girdled by a crimson
sash, charged at full speed, in solid column
and with deafening war-whoops, upon the
devoted and determined little band of heroes. Not a shot was fired by our men
until the confident and exulting savages
were within thirty yards of the rifle-pits.
Then at the word of command the Island
of Death opened, and before its unerring
aim and rapid volleys the front of the as-

saulting column halted and fell as if it had
pitched headlong against an impenetrable
wall. The rear spread away to the right
and left and sought safety in flight.

The savage was evidently dismayed and
disheartened at his sudden and crushing
repulse. The ground was strewed with
dead and dying warriors. Several bodies
were within a few yards of the breastworks. In advance of them all lay the
superb but lifeless form of Roman Nose,
the red tide from his hot veins saturating
the crimson sash which encircled his naked
body. During the siege the Indians resorted to daring by day and cunning by
night to remove these bodies, but without
success. The loss of the war-chief's life
and body was a fatal blow. The firing
almost ceased, and it was not until two
o'clock in the afternoon that another assault was attempted. It was prepared,
conducted, received, and repulsed quite
like the first one. A third, similar in
all respects, took place about four in the
afternoon; but this effort was much fee-

bler than the one which preceded it, and the gallant little band felt that it must prepare for a siege, but need not fear another assault. A September rain began, and at last the long and bloody day drew to a close and night threw a thick, wet mantle over besiegers and besieged. Not until then did the latter find time to look calmly and deliberately upon the desperate situation. Every horse and mule was killed by the enemy's fire early in the action. As the last one went down an Indian called out in audible and unbroken English, "There goes the last d—d horse down." Lieutenant Beecher, shot through the side, had died in great agony before dark. Three men, including the doctor, lay dead in the trenches; two others were mortally, and seventeen more, among them Colonel Forsyth, severely, wounded. Before ten o'clock Forsyth had been shot in the right thigh, the bullet lodging near the skin on the inner side. A few hours afterwards a ball entered his left leg below the knee, completely shattering the bone, and before night, as he was lifted up to look over the breastwork, a third bullet grazed the top of his head, making a painful scalp wound and chipping out a small piece of the skull.

The peril and location of the party were wholly unknown to their friends. Fort Wallace, the nearest point from which succor could be hoped for, was nearly a hundred miles away. Without provisions, and surrounded by more than nine hundred well-armed, well-mounted, fierce, and confident warriors, the situation was one to appall the stoutest heart. But these heroes were not daunted. The intrepid commander, forgetting his three painful wounds, from one of which he had himself cut out the ball, briefly summed up the case and gave his orders. "No shot," said he, "has been wasted ; we have plenty of ammunition, abundance of horse and mule meat, and can get water by a little digging through the sand. We will yet win the fight or sell our lives dearly in the attempt. Let a well be sunk, connect the rifle-pits by a continuous parapet, and strengthen the lines with saddles and, as far as possible, with the bodies of the dead horses. Bring in the saddle-blankets for the comfort of the wounded, and cut the horse and mule flesh into strips for food. Let two men, who are willing to risk their lives, take my rough map of the country and pocket-compass, and try to-night to steal through the enemy's line and make their way to Fort Wallace. When this is all done," he continued, "and the wounded are cared for in a secure place to be dug out for the purpose, you can rest in peace until morning, for these Indians never venture upon a night attack." The instructions were cheerfully and promptly carried out. The two scouts left the island about midnight. To escape pursuit in case they got out, they went in their stocking-feet, walking backwards, so that if the enemy discovered the tracks in the morning they might think they were made by Indians in moccasins going towards the island and not by white men leaving it. By dawn the

heroic garrison was ready for the day's
business. The scouts had not been driven
back, but there was a painful doubt as to
whether they had passed the enemy's line
or lost their lives in the attempt. All day
a steady but not destructive fire was kept
up by the Indians, and was answered
whenever it could be done with effect.
No disposition appeared to renew the desperate charges of the day before. The
Indians, exasperated by the coolness and
courage of the whites and the deliberate,
galling fire which they kept up, sought
fruitlessly, by flags of truce, pretended
withdrawals, and other devices, to draw
them from their intrenchments. Challenges and insults in the grossest language
were offered, but nothing disturbed for a
moment the caution, vigilance, and coolness of the garrison. So the day wore on,
and when night came, with raw mule-meat
alone for supper, the wounded and weary
sank to rest. Before morning two more
men started out to pass the lines and try
to bring succor. They were, however, un-

able to get through and returned. The
third day passed as the second, but the
two men who started out on the third
night did not return. The fourth day
passed as the two preceding ones. No more
scouts were sent out. The meat now began
to get putrid, and it was sprinkled with
gunpowder, in the hope that the saltpetre
in the powder would aid in preserving the
meat or make it a little less unpalatable.
But before the day was over it could no
longer be eaten, and the pangs of extreme
hunger began. A wolf that ventured too
near the lines at night was killed by a
lucky shot, and served to appease for a
short time the cravings of a few; but by
the fifth day the suffering from hunger
was intense. Then for the first time a
small fire was made of such sticks as could
be gathered together, and by charring the
putrid meat they were able to use it a little while longer. On the fifth day the Indians began to disappear, and some of the
men ventured out to gather some wild
plums near by. The plums and a jar of

pickles, which was found on the first
camp-ground, aided to sustain life. By
the seventh day the Indians had entirely
disappeared, but the beleaguered force
were now too weak to move. With no
word from their scouts, and starvation
staring them in the face, there was, with
one exception, no despondency or complaint. On the eighth day some of the
men became delirious, and the wounded
were in a dreadful condition. The shat-
tered bone of Colonel Forsyth's leg stuck
through the skin, and maggots had taken
possession of the horrible sore. The eighth
night wore away with troubled dreams of
rich feasts and wild awakenings to actual
famine. The time seemed near when neither feast nor famine could be helpful or
hurtful. Pain had almost passed away
when, on the morning of the ninth day,
men came in sight. Succor had arrived at
last; but the poor sufferers were too far
gone to cheer, or even rejoice. Perhaps
they felt instinctively that the road to relief was shorter and smoother by way of

death than by a return to life. The shrewd
and plucky scouts who left on the first
night reached Fort Wallace on the third
day thereafter, and those who got out on
the third night happened to fall in with a
scouting party of troops. Relief, which
came with all haste from both sources,
reached the fatal island at the same hour.
The stench from this contracted battle-
field was so horrible that strong men could
hardly endure it long enough to remove
the living and bury the dead.

Let us not dwell upon the painful journey to the fort, the dangerous surgical
operations, and the tedious recovery of
the wounded. The remnants of the party
which had left the post but a few days
before, full in numbers and vigor, for the
noble purpose of defending helpless women and children against the merciless
savages, returned to it with thinned ranks
and mutilated and fainting bodies, but
their high purpose had been accomplished.
Their victory was complete. They had triumphed over every weakness of body and

spirit, as well as over a most desperate
foe. If there is a lesson in the memory of
great deeds it should be found here. But,
alas ! the bright chapter which they added
to their country's glory at such heavy
cost has been passed over almost unnoted.
The empty honor of a "brevet" is the
only recognition Colonel Forsyth received
for his heroic conduct in this affair. Can
bravery, gallantry, and devotion to duty
flourish under a military system in which
such services are neither rewarded nor re-
membered ?

It is due to truth and justice to state
that in this remarkable party of fifty there
were but forty-nine heroes. The large,
knowing, and confident man on whom special reliance was placed in the beginning
utterly failed in the hour of trial. Quickly making a rifle-pit for himself, no arguments, threats, or persuasion could induce
him to rise from it or fire a shot while the
enemy was in sight. He insisted that
they always kept "a bead drawn" on
him, and that the least exposure would be

certain death.   But the loss of this man's
services was fully made up by the bravery, skill, and untiring activity of the despised "little Jew."   There was no sphere
of gallantry or usefulness in which he was
not conspicuous.

> When the foe charged on the breastworks
>   With the madness of despair,
> And the bravest souls were tested,
>   The little Jew was there.
>
> When the weary dozed on duty,
>   Or the wounded needed care,
> When another shot was called for,
>   The little Jew was there.
>
> With the festering dead around them,
>   Shedding poison in the air,
> When the crippled chieftain ordered,
>   The little Jew was there.

NOTE.—In his official report Colonel Forsyth says:
" The Indians encountered in this fight were the northern
Cheyennes, the Brulé and Ogalalla tribes of the Sioux
nation, and a band of about one hundred and seventy
'dog-soldiers,' the banditti of the various Indian tribes
on the plains.   Of their numbers it is hard to form an
estimate.   My chief scout, Abner S. Grover, since killed,
estimated the number of warriors engaged in the attack

at between eight and nine hundred. No one of the men engaged put them at less than seven hundred and fifty. Fearing, however, that I might exaggerate their numbers in my report to General Sheridan, I placed them at four hundred and fifty ; but information since obtained leads to the belief that Grover's estimate was the correct one." It may be added that two or three years after this report was made Colonel Forsyth had a long and friendly talk with some of the Indians who were engaged, and was informed by them that they had over nine hundred warriors in the fight, and lost seventy-five killed and about two hundred wounded.

"Gunnison's Massacre."

"Ah! what an unkind hour was guilty of this lamentable chance."

IT is in response to the call of duty that our regular army pioneers and protects civilization, but yet the service has its pleasures and its fascinations. To the brave and adventurous spirit it affords a rich field for enterprise and deeds of heroism. The imagination is fired by pictures of the bivouac, the social concourse around the simple meal spread upon the grass, the blazing camp-fire, the merry jest, the thrilling stories of wild adventure, cut short, perhaps, by an actual alarm. But beyond all of the romance aroused by the bright side of the picture appears a stern, and often a sad, reality.

The lonely graves of our fallen soldiers, victims to ambush, treachery, and overwhelming numbers, are scattered, unlettered and undecorated, over the Western mountains and plains. The empty saddle, the thinned ranks, or here and there a rude cross erected by the friendly hand of a comrade, tell to the brother-soldier tales of sacrifice and devotion to duty which the busy and distant world does not hear or soon forgets.

An instance of the sad fate of some of the bravest and best of our early pioneer soldiers is furnished by the official account of an exploring expedition which went into the heart of the Rocky Mountains some twenty-five years ago.

In the month of October, 1853, Captain J. W. Gunnison, of the United States Topographical Engineers, in charge of the Central Pacific Railroad Survey, being then in the vicinity of Salt Lake, Utah, received orders to proceed with a small party and a military escort to make a survey of Sevier Lake, at the head of the Sevier River, in the Rocky Mountains. But little was then known of that wild region. We were at so-called peace with

the Indian tribes and had assurances of
their friendship. The party, consisting of
Captain Gunnison ; Mr. Kern, a topo-
grapher ; Mr. Creutzfeldt, a botanist ;
Mr. Bellows, an employé ; Mr. Potter, a
Mormon guide, and an escort composed of
a lance-corporal and six privates of Company "A," Mounted Rifles, started on the
20th of October in full anticipation of a
pleasant and instructive trip. After en-
countering the friction and fatigue which
usually attend a first day's march, they
went into camp on the left of the Sevier
Lake, amid some thick willows overhang-
ing a bend of the Sevier River.

The animals were grazed and securely
picketed, supper was prepared and despatched with a relish only known thoroughly to those camping in the mountains, and, with a sentinel on post, the
weary party stretched themselves on the
ground and slept through the night un-
disturbed. In the gray of the morning
breakfast was spread upon the grass, and
just when all were gathered around it a

terrific whoop was heard from their left, and a deadly shower of bullets and arrows came from the same direction. It was a surprise, and a complete one.

Before the smoke had cleared away a band of Pah Vaut Indians (Eutaws) rushed upon them with horrid yells, and murder gleaming in their eyes. But few of the ill-fated party succeeded in reaching their arms or their horses. Those who failed to mount fell easy victims to the savage foe.

Amongst them was Captain Gunnison. Those who managed to escape carried the sad tidings with all haste to the commander of the military force encamped near Fillmore, Utah Territory, many miles away. "To horse" was sounded, and all the available troops were hastened to the scene of disaster. On the road three fugitives were met, who confirmed the tidings, but were unable to state who had fallen. Ere nightfall they came across the stripped and bloody corpses of those who had been overtaken in their

flight and murdered by the foe. Before
the fatal spot could be reached darkness
closed in, and it was impossible in that
wild and trackless region to proceed until
dawn. The troops stood to horse all
night, and at the first glimpse of day
resumed the march; but when the spot
was reached the enemy had disappeared,
and all of the remainder of Gunnison's
exploring party were found clasped in the
chilly embrace of that sleep which knows
no waking. The bodies of the captain
and the botanist were horribly mutilated,
and the wolves, as well as the savages,
had mangled the remains. Captain Gunnison had fallen by fifteen arrow-wounds,
and his left arm had been cut off at the
elbow. Thus, in the prime of life and in
time of peace, fell these noble soldiers and
faithful public servants in the zealous
and cheerful performance of an arduous
and dangerous duty. Save by their sorrowing families, and a few frontiersmen
who in their wanderings may cross the
trails or streams which bear their names,

their deeds and deaths are almost forgotten. But in the memory of the army
they still live. Deep down in its heart
dwells a lasting remembrance of beloved
comrades done to death by the treacherous foe.

Written in Blood.

THERE are men who seem born for adventure, whose every-day lives bristle with startling incidents, and who from time to time are the subjects of "disastrous chances, moving accidents, and hair-breadth 'scapes," such as those in the career of the dusky Moor of Venice, the story of which captivated the fair Desdemona.

In the army these victims of chance soon become well known as such. From the certainty with which they get wounded in battle the soldiers speak of them as "the men who try to stop all of the bullets that come along," the phrase not being intended to indicate their bravery so much as their luck. If some more dangerous and difficult enterprise than usual is to be executed, these are the ones who are certain to be picked out to lead or accompany it. If a forlorn hope is to be led, who so fit as he whose whole life has been one of danger and adventure? And yet this luck generally goes hand-in-hand with the best qualities of the soldier. The quick eye, the trained ear, the rapid thought and movement, the ready presence of mind which never fails—these are some of the advantages which the man of adventure nearly always exhibits. Such men have often seemed to baffle even death itself.

Major-General George L. Hartsuff, United States army (retired), was a remarkable example of this class. "Brought to the very verge of death five times in the direct and immediate consequence of the performance of military duty; with many scars, and with two bullets in his body received in battle; without ever having been in arrest or subjected to a reprimand; with a reputation, in short, free from spot or blemish," this gallant soldier died in New York City, May 16, 1874, from the combined powers of disease and wounds received in his country's service. His distinguished career as a commander during our great Rebellion, and his strength and fortitude in resisting pain and prostration so long as the nation was in danger, form an interesting part of the history of the mighty struggle. But to illustrate the life of United States army officers in time of *peace*, not war, is the purpose of our story. All that Hartsuff did and all that he endured in the later and more important and conspicuous part of his career was in keeping with qualities he exhibited in early life upon more contracted fields.

One of the first of them was in Florida, that "land of sun and flowers" which actual service and song and story for so many years kept fresh in the minds and memories of army men. Lieutenant Hartsuff joined his company on the Caloosahatchie in 1854. The orange-groves, pine-barrens, palmettoes, banana-trees, hummocks, and everglades which had floated in mazy confusion through his dreams when a cadet became now inviting realities. Not content with the ordinary duties of his office as lieutenant of a company, he sought and was permitted to undertake those of a topographical engineer, and pushed eagerly into the wild jungles whose mysteries had already fired his imagination. A reconnoissance of the region about the Big Cypress Swamp, with the view to the location of military roads, was the special object of the explorations. No great caution was deemed necessary. Several years had passed since we had, by de posing the chiefs who dissented, forced the Seminoles to accept a treaty requir- ing them to give up their lands and homes and to remove to the west of the Mississippi. The war which this brought on, in which our nation, operating against about three thousand men, women, and children, spent some seven years, fifteen hundred lives, and ten millions of dollars, had come to an end. Its fierce contests were over, and Osceola, the able and de- termined savage leader, caught by cunning and bad faith, had died in one of our prisons. All of his followers had been removed except the few—three hundred, perhaps—under "Billy Bowlegs," who obtained delay from time to time through promises, professions of friendliness, and other deceptions in keeping with their character and with the treatment they had received from the whites.

Lieutenant Hartsuff's surveys began in 1855. We had then been at peace (?) with the Seminoles for thirteen years. During that long period Billy Bowlegs and his followers were in constant and friendly communication with our people and troops, without, however, inspiring any great degree of confidence in their sincerity. Deep in the wilds of the marvellous region, to which they clung so fondly, these Indians had villages, where their wants, with scarce any effort on their part, were profusely supplied by nature. Game and fish were at hand and easily taken; and orange and banana trees, laden with fruit, grew without cultivation around their huts. Their villages, in fact, were not much more than luxuriant orchards serving as the rendezvous for different bands or families. They could, in all seasons, wander at pleasure in the delicious and even climate, where bud and blossom and fruit followed each other in close and unbroken procession around the circuit of the year.

To find the inhabitants all absent from these villages was not an alarming, though it was rather an unusual, occurrence. Lieutenant Hartsuff was well known to the chief, Billy Bowlegs, and to the Indians generally, and during the winter of 1854–5 he passed unmolested to and fro in their country with an escort of but one man, and frequently quite alone. Not the slightest evidence of a hostile purpose was manifested by the savages during all of that season, nor was any offence given them. The successful and valuable surveys were carried on until spring. The summer and autumn of 1855 passed quietly away, and as soon as winter set in Hartsuff, impatient for the opportunity, resumed his labors, prepared to penetrate still further into the everglades. His party was organized at Fort Myers, on the Caloosahatchie, early in December, and was enlarged with a view to so dividing it up as to cover more ground. He took one sergeant, one corporal, and eight privates, two of them acting as drivers for the two six-mule teams which formed his train, all the rest being on horseback, armed with muskets. His orders were to proceed to and reconnoitre the Big Cypress Swamp and its neighborhood. The morning of the 7th of December found the party on the march, and as the day drew to a close they encamped fifteen miles from the post, having moved slowly and encountered no adventure. After making the same distance the next day and establishing camp, a reconnoissance was made. The only persons seen were an Indian man and a boy driving hogs. They showed no hostility, tried to keep out of the way, and appeared averse to furnishing information.

The movement was continued by short marches, a part of each day, and sometimes a whole day, being devoted to careful examination of the surrounding country. Indian villages were frequently found, but no Indians and no evidence of any. Some of the old forts and block-houses built during the Florida war were found to have been burned—a fact which made Lieutenant Hartsuff more cautious, but did not deter him in the prosecution of the duty to which he had been assigned. On the 17th of December, after having been out ten days, the Lieutenant found himself in camp in the vicinity of Billy Bowlegs's village. He devoted the 18th and 19th to a thorough exploration of the neighborhood, visited several Indian villages, amongst them Billy's town and Assemwah's town, but found both these places entirely deserted. There was not the slightest evidence that a human being, civilized or savage, had been there during the preceding summer or autumn. The ripened fruit was unplucked.

The fires had long since died out. The places which had been most frequented were overrun with weeds. The long grass was tangled and knotted across the hardened but deserted paths, and silence reigned supreme in the everglades. The Seminole chief and his followers had disappeared. Their movements and purpose were matters of conjecture, the conclusion being that, for some reason known only to themselves, they had left the interior and gone to the seaboard.

A large part of the country was flooded, the water varying in depth from a few inches to five or six feet, and the entire surface being covered with grass growing from the bottom. Here and there the hummocks, slightly elevated above the general level, stood as islands, overgrown with trees, dense thickets of tropical plants, vines, thorny shrubs, etc., etc. Still higher sandy grounds were occasionally met with, timbered with large pines and quite free from underbrush, which were known as pine islands, whether surrounded by water or not. It was in a small open prairie adjoining one of these pine islands, and but a few yards in front of a hummock surrounded by its grassy lake, that Lieutenant Hartsuff's party spent the 18th and 19th of December. Neither the exploring parties during the day nor the sentinels at night discovered the least sign of Indians. This the lieutenant regretted, as, being at peace with them and having pleasant personal relations with Billy Bowlegs, the chief, he had hoped to derive valuable aid from them in making his surveys. The season being unusually wet, and having gone as far into the everglades as seemed practicable at the time, he resolved to begin his homeward march on the morning of the 20th, expecting to reach Fort Myers in time to supply the garrison for Christmas with venison and wild turkeys, of which he could kill an abundance on his return march. The night passed in perfect quiet. The guard wakened the teamsters at three A.M. ; the mules were harnessed but not hitched up ; the men

cooked and ate their breakfast, struck
their tents, and, somewhat scattered, were
by daylight in the act of saddling their
horses — the lieutenant's breakfast was
ready at the camp-fire, while he, but partly dressed, was yet in his tent—when the
war-whoop from forty savage throats rent
the still air, and a shower of bullets crash-
ed among the startled little band. Every
tree in the adjacent pine island sheltered a
warrior, the nearest of them being but a
few feet distant. The Indians, as is their
usual practice on such occasions, directed
their efforts to destroying or stampeding
the animals. The fire they concentrated
upon the teams made it difficult for the
men to assemble under cover of the wagons. Three out of the ten enlisted men
—the sergeant, the corporal, and one private — who were saddling their horses a
short distance away, were cut off from the
main body and took no part in the struggle. They alone escaped unhurt. At the
sound of the first whoop the lieutenant,
seizing his revolver and rushing out of his

tent, saw the foe, painted and fantastically adorned, advancing stealthily from the cover of one tree to that of another. He quickly shot two of them who were almost within reach of the muzzle of his pistol; then, receiving a severe wound in his arm, he ran to the wagons, a few yards distant, passing on the way two of his men who had fallen mortally wounded. At the wagons he found two others lying dead, but three brave fellows were fighting desperately under such shelter as the wagons afforded. One of these, like himself, was already badly wounded. But while the lieutenant and this soldier were prevented by their wounds from loading, they were able to fire, and this they did as rapidly as the other two prepared the surplus muskets for their use. The unequal struggle was of short duration. But two soldiers were on their feet, and both of these were wounded. The lieutenant, in addition to the wound in his arm, had received a severe and intensely painful shock from a bullet which struck a pistol

in his pocket, and by the time he rallied
from this a ball penetrated his side and
lodged in his lung, where, years after, it
formed the centre of the inflammation
from which he died.   He told the two
surviving men he could do nothing more
and they must take care of themselves,
and hastened to the cover of the adjacent
hummock.   The two wounded soldiers followed, and, after great suffering, reached
Fort Myers.   While the facts were still
fresh, one of them—a rough but gallant
fellow — gave his commander a written
account, from which the following are
extracts :

"The lieutenant was dressed, had washed, and was, I think, combing his hair,
when I heard the war-whoop and a shot
fired.   I was getting his breakfast and
didn't know what it meant ; thought it
was our men firing at a deer, until I
saw an Indian behind a tree in act of firing.
Soon as I saw that I seized and fired
my rifle and retreated to the wagons for
shelter.   There I found Hanna and Mur-

taugh. We fired two rounds each, when Murtaugh received a wound through the belly and fell. He exclaimed, 'I am mortally wounded.' I told him to get into a hummock and save himself, and he did so. Lieutenant Hartsuff then ran up and said: 'For God's sake, where are all the men? Were they all killed at first fire?' I answered: 'These two are all I have seen.' He then asked: 'How are you off for ammunition?' I said: 'Pretty short.' It was about this time that Hanna was shot in the stomach and myself in the thigh, but the ball or slug struck my knife and saved my leg. I heard the lieutenant say that Foster or Worth had a leg broke; also that if we could get to shelter we could lick them all. He asked us to load for him and hand him muskets, which he fired several times until he received a shot in the left side; it made him stagger clear around. He put his hand to his side and said he was done for, paused two minutes, pulled out his pistol, and said: 'Now, by heavens! the pistol has saved my life, for

the ball has struck the pistol.' He was
also shot in the left side. Being exhausted from loss of blood, he shortly afterwards
retreated to a hummock. Myself and Hanna fired three or four shots more, and I
said to him: 'My last cartridge is in my
rifle, and our legs must save us.' He
answered me. Then we retreated to a
hummock, and put off in direction of Fort
Simon Drum, going a good deal out of
our course, thinking they would pursue
us on horseback. Both of us together
made the best of our way to Fort Myers.
I arrived on the evening of the 21st,
having walked the whole distance, seventy
miles, about fifty of which were knee-
deep in water, carrying my rifle, and
without eating a mouthful of food. I
left Baker, who had his rifle also, about
fifteen miles from Fort Myers, he having become so exhausted as to be unable to walk further." Lieutenant Hartsuff was now alone and desperately wounded. He with great effort crawled through
the hummock, but in crossing a "lily-

pond" fell and was unable to rise again, the water covering all but his head. While in this position he heard an Indian cry: "Come out, come out!" He remained perfectly quiet, and the Indians, possibly awed by the gallantry he had displayed and his mysterious disappearance from their view, quickly left the field with their ill-gotten plunder. And now commenced a struggle for life, possibly never equalled for endurance and persistency. Lieutenant Hartsuff remained in the pond where he had fallen for about two hours. The agony from his wounds was intense, and the alligators, attracted by his blood, made his position doubly dangerous. He got up and staggered along about two hundred yards, when he fell from exhaustion. He remained on the ground, unable to move, until night, when he dragged his suffering body inch by inch for about half a mile, when exhausted nature again succumbed, and, blistered by the hot sun and lacerated by thorns and briers, he again fell, and lay in mortal agony for two

days and two nights. On the evening of
the third day he managed to get to his
feet, and slowly staggered on towards Fort
Simon Drum. He could only go about
half a mile at a time ; but his wonderful
vitality held him up, and slowly but surely
he made his way. In this manner he pro-
gressed until sunrise, but could then go
no further. He lay down, and fortunately found water close by, with which he re-
freshed his parched lips and laved his
fevered brow. Food had not passed his
lips for eighty-two hours. He remained in
this place until the following afternoon
(Sunday), when he again resumed his
weary journey, and finally approached the
Fort, and was found by a party of soldiers
in search of him at about eight o'clock in
the evening. During his journey he had,
from time to time, bound and rebound his
own wounds, and, when he had almost
given up hope, had written his name and
a brief account of the disaster on a small
piece of paper with his own blood, and this
paper was found pinned to his breast.

His strong constitution, wonderful nerve, and impatience of the tediousness of the sick-room all combined to produce a quick recovery; and Lieutenant Hartsuff took the field in the following spring against the same Indians who had so nearly destroyed him in the winter.

It is not our purpose to treat of his subsequent glorious career, but merely to give an example of unsurpassed bravery and endurance. All are tenacious of life, but to all it is not given to defy death as did this hero. When we recollect that not only had he to contend against the pain of severe wounds, but against the quite as deadly pangs of hunger and of thirst, we can but wonder of what stuff this brave soul was made. But in after-years, on other fields more in the public gaze and with greater opportunities for glory, he showed that it was forged of the true metal, and that time had but tempered the steel and hardened it for his country's service. He was a Titan in body as in mind, and "though gone before he is not forgotten."

"Soldiers Afloat."

OUR war with Mexico ended in 1848,
giving us California; the Pacific
Railroad was still an embryo in
the womb of the future, and rude stage-
coaches and more primitive vehicles were
the only means of conveyance overland.
The alternative was the long voyage
around the Horn. The line between our
possessions and those of Great Britain
in the Northwest had, after great discussion and display of temper, been finally
decided.

It was deemed necessary by our Government to take military possession of our
Pacific regions; accordingly, a battalion
of the First Regiment of United States
Artillery, consisting of companies "L"
and "M," the former commanded by Captain and Brevet-Major Hathaway and the

latter by Captain Hill, received orders on the 12th of September, 1848, to proceed to Oregon and establish the military posts required on that line. An officer of one of the companies selected for this expedition, being asked many years afterwards to give a short account of the voyage to that distant and unexplored region, wrote as follows:

Shakspeare divides the life of man into seven ages. But the life of a soldier naturally, almost inevitably, further subdivides itself into well-defined parts ; campaigns in active operations and new stations in time of peace forming distinct chapters, complete in themselves, and, like the acts in a drama, each having its own scenery and *dramatis personæ*. To recur to these chapters after they have gone into the past is usually interesting and always more or less instructive. How often do we wonder at the false notions, the selfishness, and possibly the partisanship with which we played our parts ! How utterly unworthy of the importance which we

once attached to them those parts may now
seem, and how valuable such reflections
might be if we could apply them properly
to the affairs of the present, which are but
making up another chapter, soon, like the
rest, to become a part of the past! One of
these chapters in my life ended with the
close of the Mexican war, and another began with assignment to a battalion of the
First United States Artillery, ordered on
the 12th of September, 1848, to proceed
from New York City, *via* Cape Horn, to
the Columbia River in Oregon. A long
and delightful tour of duty at Fort Hamil-
ton was in prospect when the unexpected
summons came, entailing a six months'
sea-voyage and a prolonged stay in the
wilderness at the end of it. California
was secured to us by the treaty of "Gua-
dalupe Hidalgo," and troops had been sent
into that region. Our bluster about "fifty-
four-forty or fight" had ceased, and we
had accepted *forty-nine* as our northern
boundary of Oregon, and in 1849 a Terri-
torial government was established and

that region was organized into military department No. 2. A battalion of the First United States Artillery was directed to take military possession. In preparing the battalion for this expedition the married officers were replaced by unmarried ones. The tour of duty was to be a protracted one in a field where it was supposed no marriageable ladies could be found. The question whether, under the circumstances, married or unmarried officers ought to be selected, was fully and earnestly discussed, the married men taking the negative. They made their point, though it was never admitted that they settled a principle. Owing, probably, to the action in this connection, six, if not seven, of the nine " flowers " who constituted this command "wasted their sweetness on the desert air " and remained bachelor soldiers.

The battalion went on board the Government transport *Massachusetts*, a full-rigged ship, with a propeller as an auxiliary, on the 10th of November, 1848. How

I dreaded meeting the medical officer of the command! There was a coolness between us. In the winter of 1847 I went to the city of Mexico in charge of a detachment of recruits for the Third United States Artillery. On the day of arrival two or three of the recruits were sick. The acting sergeant of the detachment was directed to present them to the doctor next morning. The surgeon resided in the city and came to the presidio at sick-call. The sick of the regular garrison were presented to him by the orderly sergeants of companies, their names on a sick-book in due form. After these were all disposed of on the morning in question, the sick recruits were brought forward with their names written on a dirty slip of paper. The doctor would not recognize them; cut them off short—no sick-book, did not know who they were, etc.—and they received no physic. This was reported, and I said to the doctor, using a slang expression familiar to West Point, and probably putting on some extra airs, "Well, doctor,

you 'cut' my recruits this morning." A
few words of explanation followed, but the
doctor soon gave me to understand that he
knew his own business, and if I had a complaint it must be made officially. I there-
upon left him. The matter, however,
seemed to sour on his mind. The next
morning he attended to my recruits, and to
me too. He prescribed pills for them and
powder for me. I was struck with amaze-
ment. I read and re-read his note without
being able to understand just what my offence was. It *seemed* to be not so much
what I had said or done as that the saying
and doing were by a very young officer. I
can see plainly now that the doctor and I
were looking from entirely different stand-
points. He was comparing me with the
officers of high rank, gallant services, and
great knowledge with whom he was in
daily association, and he therefore expected a large degree of modesty, deference, and respect, whereas my mind was
entirely filled by certain great truths obtained from another direction, and was

totally closed to the considerations which
occupied his. I looked downwards to the
level I had left and compared myself with
the cadets ; in doing so I felt that I had
reached a dizzy height. I *had just graduated at West Point;* had "changed the
gray for the blue" ; was in actual possession of the dazzling prize which the instructor once held up before the gaze of
the flagging cadet. I was receiving in my
own hands sixty-four dollars and fifty
cents a month, and had a red stripe down
the leg of my trousers. I *could* not under
these circumstances be modest, and did
not feel that I owed deference to anybody.
Graduates of the Military Academy will
understand the feeling it is designed to
describe. By a happy chance I determined to put the whole matter into the
hands of the older officers of my regiment
and abide by their judgment. While they
were perfectly willing to perform the disagreeable duty of taking the conceit out of
their own subs, they were not at all in-
clined to let an outsider, especially a staff-

officer, have a hand in it, or even to ac-
knowledge to outsiders that there was any
conceit to be dealt with. They prepared a
very weak and diplomatic letter of explanation for my signature. The doctor accepted the same and dropped the subject,
but he dropped me with it. We were
strangers to each other until we met on
the deck of the old *Massachusetts* as officers *en route* to Oregon. Then he gave me
his hand in a frank and cordial way. He
had evidently, with good sense and good
taste, placed the incident where it belonged, in the closed chapter on the Mexican war.

While the lieutenants of the command
had well-defined characteristics, there was
no one so peculiar as to be offensive, or
even disagreeable, to the others. One was
a practical joker, who put emetics in his
whiskey when he found the steward was
stealing it. Another was the wag, as far
as we permitted that character to develop.
Another still was the banker, who lent us
money when we were hard up. We placed

no restriction upon the development of *his* specialty. To meet our expenses in foreign ports we were permitted to draw six months' pay in advance, *and most of us spent it in advance.* I advise no one to repeat this part of my experience.

The *Massachusetts*, Captain Wood commanding, had ample accommodations. The men were comfortably quartered between decks, and each officer had a state-room. The captain of the ship furnished waiters for the cabin and meals for the officers at a very reasonable rate. Twice a week one of the officers used to say that he had dined out. These were our days for "plum-duff," which he would partake of freely for the purpose of producing the feeling of discomfort and distension of the stomach, which he said was the principal result of dinner-parties with him. The officers had their own servants. In those days one servant attended to two or three officers, and did it well. Now it takes two or three servants to wait on one officer. It is difficult to say exactly what this change

should be attributed to. Perhaps it has
been brought about by the spirit of *organization,* which is one of the hobbies of the
present age. Organization and reorganization are now carried into all the concerns
of life, great and small, and are frequently
resorted to with no other result than en-
abling *somebody* to escape the full and fair
share of the work which actually belongs
to him. In domestic affairs of the present
day organization means getting one more
servant to wait on those already employed.
My servant was Bill, a colored boy fifteen
years old. He was brought up in Church
Street, New York, and came to me well
recommended (they always do). Bill had
certain vices which it is very difficult for
an employer to distinguish from virtues,
especially during active operations or at
remote places. He preyed upon the rest
of the world for the benefit of his master
and himself.

It takes a person of some experience
and cultivation always to draw the line
between *foraging* and *stealing* just in the

right place.   Bill failed in it.   His master
had no money but the little he borrowed,
yet in Rio Janeiro Bill had plenty.   In
Valparaiso he was flush.   In Honolulu he
was positively lavish.   After leaving the
last-named port our commissary and quar-
termaster counted his public funds.   He
started with ten thousand dollars in coin,
deposited in a small iron chest which he
kept in his stateroom.   The count showed
a considerable deficiency.   An investigation was held and search made without
developing any significant facts, but every-
body felt sure Bill was guilty.   Flogging
seemed to be regarded as a necessary feature in so long a voyage, and it was decided by the authorities to flog Bill until
he confessed.   He was accordingly tied up
in the rigging and the lash was applied,
but he denied to the last and was released
with the sympathies of his tormentors.
Very soon afterwards, however, accident
exposed his guilt, and he made full confession and explanation.   He had managed
to get hold of the key, and had been run-

ning his arm elbow-deep into our minia-
ture United States Treasury. This was
thirty years ago. He was a little in advance of his generation. Bill was put
ashore at the mouth of the Columbia
River without a recommendation. He
did not need one. Some time after he was
seen in the streets of San Francisco, smil-
ing and prosperous. They had evidently
not yet found him out. He subsequently
disappeared suddenly and was heard of
no more. Justice was swift and sure in
California when they had no law there.
He probably shared the fate of the man
whose profession and end a Missouri poet
describes as follows :

> "He found a rope and picked it up,
>   And with it walked away ;
>   It happened that to t'other end
>   A horse was hitched, they say.
>
> " *They* found a tree and tied the rope
>   Unto a swinging limb ;
>   It happened that the other end
>   Was somehow hitched *to him*."

To return from this long digression,

We sailed out of New York harbor on Friday, the 10th of November, 1848. It was a cold and dreary day. Summer had started south several weeks before, but we caught up in a few days and carried it with us through both the northern and southern waters of the Atlantic and Pacific. During the entire voyage the general rules governing troops on board transports were strictly observed, and all of the ordinary military duties which the limited space would permit were performed. The companies were regularly paraded, inspected, mustered, and drilled at the manual of arms ; guard-mounting was conducted in due form and guard duty rigidly performed. Sunday inspections were rather more thorough than in garrison. The Episcopal service was read by the captain of the ship.

We reached Rio Janeiro early in December. Here, as at other stopping-places on the voyage, we attracted attention as the first body of United States Regulars that had appeared upon the scene.

Our navy was strongly represented in
the harbor of Rio Janeiro, and was active
and vigilant in its efforts to suppress that
greatest of all infamies, the slave trade.
Immediately after arrival we had our first,
in fact our only, disturbance on ship-
board. It seems there was at that time
something in the unwritten law prescrib-
ing the duties and privileges of sailors
under which the crew expected, part at a
time, to have a run on shore immediately
after getting into port. For reasons which
he deemed sufficient the captain decided
that water must be taken aboard before
any of the men could leave the ship. The
sailors struck—every man of them refused
to go to work. The captain applied to
the battalion commander for aid in enforcing discipline. A military guard was paraded on the quarter-deck, all hands called
aft, and the sailors formed in line in front
of the guard. The captain, solemn and
determined, was in front of his crew.
With the guard behind them he knew he
had the best of it. The first mate stood

by with a small handful of lashing cords;
the second mate near the mainstay with a
"cat" in his hand; the third mate near
him with another "cat" to meet the con-
tingency of the second mate getting tired
or sick. There was no speech-making, no
remonstrance, no explanation. The captain said, addressing himself directly to
the sailor on the right of the line:
"Jack, will you go to duty?" Jack answered: "No, sir." "Trice him up in the
main rigging and flog him until he says
he will go to his duty." The first mate
"triced" accordingly, and the second mate
flogged. After about a dozen lashes Jack
said: "I will go to me duty, sir," and
he was taken down and sent forward.
The same course was pursued with every
one of the eighteen or twenty sailors. It
seemed to be a part of their *noblesse* that
every man should take his flogging before yielding, and their pluck—and probably rank among themselves in the fore-
castle—was fixed by the relative amounts of
punishment endured before surrendering.

Some took twenty or thirty blows, whereas others gave in at the third or fourth.
The case of one sailor indicated that there
was no statute of limitation in the code of
the ship. After he announced that he
would go to duty the second mate said:
"This man was sulky and impudent during the gale just after we left New York.
Can I give him a few for that, sir?" The
captain simply replied: "Aye, aye, sir,"
and the mate settled old scores according
to his own judgment without further
discussion or explanation. As soon as
these ceremonies were over the crew went
to work cheerfully enough pumping water
aboard, and at the order of the first mate,
who sang out, "Come, start a song there,
some of ye," they actually began to sing.
It is hoped this incident will not be regarded as furnishing an argument in favor
of flogging. It may be a little amusing,
but the occurrence exhibited a lamentable
brutality in more directions than one.

We sailed from Rio Janeiro soon after
Christmas for the Straits of Magellan, as,

by means of our propeller, we could make
the smoother and more interesting trip
through the Straits instead of the rougher
and more tedious one around the Horn.
Not knowing much about the navigation
of that narrow passage, we ran only by
day, and not every day, as both a strong
wind and current, setting from the Pacific
to the Atlantic side, made navigation difficult and unsafe. We were a week going
through, and saw nothing of special interest. A few native Indians of the very
lowest order, whose desire for tobacco was
the only thing they could make known to
us, and the guards of a penal station
which Chili has about the middle of the
Straits, were the only persons we encountered. It was mid-summer in that region,
but the weather was cold and windy, with
snow in the air. From the Straits of Magellan we went to Valparaiso, where we
spent six days most delightfully. One
evening while in that city we dined
ashore with some officers of our navy.
They were all jolly good fellows. We

were to join our barge at twelve midnight to go on board. The good cheer
and pleasant company had made us merry.
We could not see much, it being rather
dark; but everything we did see was beau-
tiful. One of our lieutenants found a
Skye terrier on a doorstep. He confiscated
it, claiming that we were in an enemy's
country, as shown by the fact that the inhabitants spoke Spanish, the language of
our enemies, the Mexicans. After some
perseverance with his burden he reached
the wharf. Having been several months
afloat, and just from dinner with seafaring
men, we felt bound to indulge freely in
nautical language. The lieutenant called
out: "I say, cox'ain, stand by to take a
dog aboard." "Aye, aye, sir," replied
the coxswain. "Away *she* goes," said the
lieutenant, (it was a male, but sailors are
partial to the feminine gender.) The lieutenant generated much force for "heav-
ing" the animal, but, instead of applying
it all to the dog, he divided it between the
dog's body and his own about in proportion

to their respective masses.   The dog went into the boat and the lieutenant went into the sea.   The coxswain was equal to the occasion.   He sang out : "Man overboard. Stand by, all hands, to catch *her* as *she* rises."   "Hold fast there, you, Jack ; keep all ye get."   (A sailor had seized the lieutenant by the hair as he came to the surface.)   "All together now ! *haul !* steady ! lower away on her !" and the lieutenant was stretched in the bottom of the barge. "There ye are, *sir*."   The lieutenant's gender was restored as soon as the coxswain's duty of "hauling" and "lowering away" on him had been completed.   After his plunge-bath the youngster took a more sober view of things.   The Skye terrier had changed into a mangy, short-haired cur.   It was pitched on to the wharf without any nautical phrases, and thus escaped either a watery grave or a captivity which, no doubt, would have proved equally disagreeable to captive and captor.   At Valparaiso we heard for the first time of the discovery of gold in California.   The

stories were marvellous, but, as we learned
subsequently, were not exaggerated. We
had thought of making San Francisco our
next stopping-place, but the danger of
losing both sailors and soldiers decided us,
on leaving Valparaiso, February 15, 1849,
to shape our course for the Sandwich
Islands. On our way there we passed
over some good, so-called, whaling *grounds*
near the Galapagos Islands. New Bed-
ford was there in force. We were boarded
by one captain who had been in those
waters for nearly three years, and during
all that time had received no news from
home. The fact of Taylor's election to the
Presidency of the United States had been
announced just as we were leaving New
York. We sailed big with the news,
and gladly retailed it upon every opportunity. When the whaler came aboard
we waited only for suitable questions to
surprise and interest him ; but, Yankee
though he was, he asked no questions,
and we were compelled to volunteer our
information. It did not seem to interest

him in the least. We offered him the latest New York papers, which he accepted politely, but in a way that showed they were of no value to him. Nothing aroused him until he saw a signal from his vessel that a whale was spouting. Then he showed the man and master. His leave-taking was a hasty one. He probably felt so far behind in the matter of news as to make him conclude it would be a hopeless task to try and get enough during this visit to understand what we were talking about. His heart and mind were evidently impervious to everything except getting his cargo of oil and going home. Under the circumstances this was doubtless the happiest condition he could be in. What a wise provision of nature that enabled him to reach it!

Arriving at Honolulu on the 9th of April, 1849, we were objects of interest and wonder to the natives. But one *steamer* before ours had entered the port, and that was not seen by the king and queen of the islands. Our troops were the

first that had ever appeared there, and,
no doubt, in numbers and appointments
looked to the natives like a large and
thoroughly equipped *army*. The Hawai-
ian Government had a very small military
force in the town. We were treated with
marked kindness and politeness by the
king, princes, and ministers. We sailed from Honolulu on the 15th of April,
1849, for the mouth of the Columbia
River, arriving off the harbor on the 9th
of May. The bar was difficult and dangerous even with a pilot. The breakers
showed all the way across. The channel
going in ran first about east, then nearly
north, and then east again, requiring two
sharp turns in close quarters. We stood off
and on during the 9th, studying the bear-
ings, and on the 10th decided to venture
in. Our captain spread his charts before
him ; desired that every one should be
still and silent; got on a full head of
steam and approached the bar; but instead of entering, his courage oozed out
and he turned off to sea. He wanted an

infusion of pluck. He said to the commanding officer of the troops: "Major,
do you order me to go over that bar?"
The major replied: "Captain, where do
the written instructions under which you
have come thus far require you to go?"
The captain said: "Into the Columbia
River." "That is just where mine require me to go with you, and the sooner
you take me there the better I shall like
it," said the major. "But," said the captain, "are you prepared to take the risk
of being lost on that bar?" "I am prepared," said the major, "to ride in this
ship wherever you are prepared to drive
her in pursuance of your instructions to
land me in the Columbia River." That ended the interview between the chief soldier
and sailor ; but a loud murmur ran around
among the officers of the battalion. "Oh !
go ahead, captain," they said; "you can
make it, there is no danger," and so
forth. That bar was all that lay between
us and the end of a long voyage. We
were tired of looking upon the sea, of

smelling bilge-water, of eating corned
beef and "plum-duff." It was a lovely
day in May, and the land-breeze brought
sweet odors from the shore. The tall
firs and patches of green sward were
plainly visible to the naked eye; and
through the glass we could see men and
women (Indians) enjoying the freedom of
the forest. Any danger seemed prefer-
able to delay. With nerve and skill that
did him honor, the captain finally made
the venture and carried his ship over
safely, and landed us at Fort Vancouver,
about one hundred and thirty miles up
the river, on the 13th of May, 1849.
We established our camp on a ridge
in the edge of the wood; by great
labor trimmed all the branches from a
straight fir-tree more than a hundred
and fifty feet high, fixed a pulley on the
top, and hoisted the stars and stripes.
We had reached the end of our long
voyage. It had been a safe and pleasant
one, notwithstanding the fact that it was
begun on *Friday*. We had not lost a

man by death or desertion. Not an officer had been put in arrest or under
charges.   There had been but little drinking and no gambling, (there was *some*
card-playing after the rifle regiment arrived in the following autumn.) No quar-
rel or miff occurred among us during the
six months' voyage, (there were no ladies on board.) To narrate the events of
our stay in Oregon would take too long,
and perhaps prove tedious. Suffice it
to say both officers and men found the
country charming. Besides hunting, fish-
ing, boating, riding, etc., we had all the
novelty of a comparatively new world to
interest us.

Of the nine officers who belonged to
this battalion, but one is left upon the
active list of the army. One is on the
retired list. Two are engaged in civil
pursuits, having resigned many years
ago. Five have gone to their graves;
they are mourned as truest of the true
among their friends. Admiration, pre-
ference, love even, may be given without

thorough acquaintance, and those senti-
ments are often independent of the *worthiness* of the object. But *true friendship*, that which cannot decay or be
broken, is based upon that thorough
knowledge of each other which is acquired only under peculiar circumstances.
Friendships formed in the times that
"try men's souls" are enduring, because
founded upon convictions of worthiness
that venial faults cannot impair.

"The Penitentes."

A N officer of the army, travelling on
duty in New Mexico during the summer of 1877, took occasion to make
some researches into the habits and customs of that region, especially of the de-
scendants of the Spaniards who formerly
held possession of the territory. None
more curious were observed than those of
the religious sect of "The Penitentes."

These are persons who belong to a secret
religious order existing in both Old and
New Mexico. The origin of the fraternity
is not well defined, but there is not much
doubt that it has grown up in New Mexico
since the Spaniards took possession in
1540 and enforced the Roman Catholic religion upon the inhabitants, the Pueblo
Indians. Indian superstition may, to some
extent, have crept into this monstrosity;

but the order itself is an outgrowth of the
Church of Rome as administered by the
Spaniards. The dogma of that Church
under which penances were exacted and
indulgences granted is probably the corner-
stone of the sect. "Penitentes" are Roman-
ists; but in both Old and New Mexico there
are many members of the Church who do
not belong to the order. In fact, the Church
professes not to encourage the order; but
it tolerates it, yielding to what it cannot
now prevent, even if it would. This tole-
ration is shown in many ways; as, for example, keeping the doors of the church
open to permit the "Penitentes," when
coming in procession from secret meetings
at their lodges, to enter and complete their
ceremonies at the foot of the altar.

The superstitions and cruelties of this
remarkable sect are so gross that it could
not maintain its existence by recruiting its
ranks from an adult population as inferior
even as that of which it is now composed.
Occasionally an adult joins, but membership is generally acquired by inheritance—

children receiving it from their parents by
birth, and being brought up to the observance of its duties. At the tender age of
ten or eleven years females as well as
males are initiated in its most cruel prac-
tices. The members in New Mexico are
necessarily nearly all natives ; but the order does not restrict membership to any
one nationality. An Irishman once joined,
but whether Pat acted from conviction,
curiosity, or pure devilment does not appear. Two "Yankees" also are known to
have been initiated for the characteristic
purpose, as it was alleged, of securing the
political favor of the brotherhood. Mutual aid in case of necessity is one of the
obligations, probably the best, of membership. Penances vary with offences, and
are not always the same for the same sins.
They change with attending circumstances,
and also with the localities, the greatest
cruelties being practised in those places
where the people are most ignorant and
superstitious. Conspicuous ceremonies
take place several times during the year,

but those of Holy Week are the most
striking. The following affords a fair example of them :

There are two lodges of Penitentes at La
Junta, New Mexico, about two miles from
Fort Union. A lodge is usually an adobe
structure, rectangular in shape and some
twenty feet square ; one story high, with
one door ; near the roof one small square
window with a wooden shutter. On Thurs-
day in Holy Week of 1877 the members
were assembled in one of their lodges, door
and window closed. A quarter of a mile
or so from the lodge stood a full-sized
crucifix. About noon the lodge door
opened and a procession emerged. It consisted of a column of three single files.
The outer files, each more numerous than
the centre one, were made up of attendants. The centre file was composed of nine
persons, who were the "penitentes" of the
occasion. Six were men, one a woman,
and two were boys of about ten or twelve
years of age. The men and boys were
naked, except that each wore a pair of

linen trousers. The woman wore but one
garment, and that hung loosely from her
shoulders to her ankles. The faces of
all were concealed by handkerchiefs,
scarfs, or masks. Some of the men
carried on their backs crosses made of
green timber about a foot square, the long
arm being some fourteen or fifteen feet,
the whole making a weight which it was
just possible for the bearer to carry by
stooping and clasping his arms around
the short arm of the cross, while the lower
end of the long arm dragged on the ground.
The boys, and the men who did not bear
crosses, carried in their hands long scourges made of the "soapweed," a species of
cactus, plaited into an instrument of torture not less severe than a "cat-o'-nine
tails." Before leaving the lodge the backs
of the unfortunate sufferers were scarified
with sharp pieces of flint. This was done
not so much to add to the sufferings as
to make the blood flow freely under the
tortures yet to come, and thus prevent
the serious consequences which might

otherwise follow the clotting of blood and bruising of the flesh by the scourge. The woman's preparations were for even deeper agony than that of her companions. On her naked back, beneath the gown, she wore a round, thorny cactus plant, about the diameter of an ordinary water-pail and some six or eight inches thick ; her hands were pinioned behind, her ankles tied together by a cord which permitted her to take steps of only six inches at a time ; about her neck a rope was fastened with its two ends extending to the front, each end being held by an attendant. Thus prepared, the ghastly procession dragged its slow pace along, the Penitentes, one behind the other, two or three yards apart. The route was that leading to the standing cross in the distance. The progress was attended with the loud noise of chants, moans, and lamentations. The cross-bearers frequently fell upon their faces under their crushing burdens, and were as often helped to their feet by the zealous attendants, only to stag-

ger on and fall again. At every step
those with scourges lashed their bleeding
backs with all the force of both hands,
first over one shoulder and then over the
other. The blood flowed in streams to
their feet, saturating the white trousers.
The lacerated backs soon became raw and
skinless masses, the scourges growing more
and more severe as they hardened by taking up blood and flesh. The woman, hob-
bled as she was, and with her hands lashed
to her back, bore against the rope held by
the two attendants in front. These now
and again, by sudden jerks, threw her full
length upon the ground, with the thorny
cactus on her back and no protection from
her pinioned hands. After these falls she
was lifted to her feet again, only to suf-
fer a repetition of this most astounding
cruelty. When the procession at length
reached the cross all knelt, or tried to
kneel. Many of the Penitentes, on drop-
ping to their knees, fell prostrate to the
earth under their sufferings and their
heavy burdens. The ceremonies at the

cross, noisy and meaningless to the un-
initiated, consumed some fifteen or twenty
minutes. Then the procession reformed
and went back in the same manner that it
came. The attendants during the return
had more frequently to raise and drag the
fallen victims, and some of them even
seized and plied the scourges, which, from
agony and exhaustion, the sufferers were
using too gently. When the lodge was at
last entered, the door was closed and the
infliction of torture came to an end. These
barbarous rites were followed by wild
ceremonies in the lodge at night, intended
to symbolize the casting off of sin which
had been effected by the agonies of the
day. At midnight the members moved in
slow procession to the church, whose por-
tals they found open to them, and there
closed the performances for the time being.

Actual crucifixion sometimes forms part
of the rites of which the foregoing is
an illustration. The choice of the victim
does not depend either on his virtues or
his vices. He is selected by lot, and is

deemed peculiarly fortunate. The crown
of thorns, spear, and nails are omitted; but
exhaustion and the stoppage of circulation, produced by the tightly-drawn liga-
ments with which he is lashed to the cross,
sometimes produce death. The sufferer
is kept on the cross until the ceremonials
around the foot of it are completed. His
moans from above are drowned by louder
noises from below, and his condition goes
unheeded. If he holds out, well and
good; if not, so much the worse for him.
Deaths from sufferings on the cross, as well
as from those during the procession, have
occurred quite recently. When they hap-
pen the body is quickly covered by the
attendants, carried off and quietly buried,
and silence is kept. No one appears to
have ever yet cared enough about such
losses to start investigation or enquiry
concerning them.

The parts taken by the sufferers in these
sacrificial rites usually result from some
general rule or scale fixed by the lodge;
but sometimes they are by special decision.

In either case they may arise from confession or conviction.

When a Penitente dies the funeral is conducted according to the forms of the church ; but prior to, and independent of, the funeral, the order holds a species of "wake" over the remains at the residence of the deceased. Friends assemble at night, the members of the order alone being admitted to the room where the services of the sect are performed. These services consist of lamentations, prayers, and scourging of the naked backs of the men of the family. Their dwellings are low, and the scourges used on these occasions often reach the ceilings and bedaub them with blood from the backs of the mourners.

The tenets of this peculiar sect are handed down orally from generation to generation. Whether the tortures they inflict are endured as atonement for sins of the past or to secure indulgence for those of the future, or with an eye in both directions, is not known to the world. It is quite probable that the gross cruelties are enforced merely as superstitions without any very well defined purpose. There is certainly nothing specially reformatory in the torture. The members of the order are no better than the rest of the community, if as good. Possibly they imagine their sufferings close old accounts of sin and permit the opening of new ones, even if they do not create a balance to the credit of the sinner. Certainly they go on sinning quite as freely after as they did before the settlement.

It is astonishing that in these days of missionaries and Christian labor such a condition of things should exist in our land. It illustrates the heterogeneous character of our population; but the picture has no bright or humorous side.

"The Fatal Valley."

"A nation's gratitude perchance may spread
A thornless pillow for the widow's head ;
May lighten well her heart's maternal care,
And wean from penury the soldier's heir."

IN the annals of our Indian warfares,
filled as they are with accounts of
atrocities perpetrated by the savage
red-man, none more heartrending is to
be found than the horrible massacre of
Brevet Lieutenant-Colonel W. J. Fetterman, Captain F. H. Brown, and Lieutenant Grummond, with forty-nine men of
the Eighteenth United States Infantry,
and twenty-seven men of the Second
United States Cavalry, and two civilians
as volunteers, on the 21st of December,
1866, in the vicinity of Fort Philip
Kearney, Dakota Territory. This post
and Fort C. F. Smith, to the northwest

of it, both established in the summer
of 1866, in the best and almost the last
hunting-ground of the Sioux, were rank-
ling thorns in the side of this large and
warlike nation. The savages saw that
the purpose was to open and protect a
road from Virginia City, Montana, to the
settlements in the East, thus bisecting
their haunts. Unfortunately, there was
not a proper relation between the strength
of these remote stations * and the danger
to which they were exposed. The white
man had not yet lost any of the confidence inspired by years of almost unvary-
ing triumph over the savage.†

He still entertained the mistaken notion
that his long-continued success was due
mainly to his personal superiority as a
warrior over the despised foe, and not to
the better weapons with which he was

* General Sherman's annual report, dated October 1, 1867, says
the post of Fort Phil. Kearney was "garrisoned by five companies of
the Eighteenth Infantry and one company of the Second Cavalry—four
hundred and eleven men present for duty."

† Colonel Carrington, in his official report of this affair, says : "The
officers who fell believed that no Indian force could overwhelm that
number of troops well held in hand."

armed. But the time of bows and arrows
as the Indian's war armament had gone or
was rapidly passing away. While we
were fully occupied from 1861 to 1865 with
the war of the Rebellion, the swarms of
savages on the frontiers were providing
themselves on easy terms with the best
of arms from the white man's stores.
The supply of ammunition was so abundant that its use was no longer limited
to killing game for food, but could be
extended to battles, and even protracted
campaigns, against those who furnished it.
The Indian realized before the white man
did that his old disadvantage was due to
his arms and not to his personality. That
very knowledge made him a stronger man.
He could always greatly outnumber us in
any combat in which he chose to engage,
and, being as well armed as the white
man, he was no longer influenced by
doubts as to the result of any hostile enterprise he deemed it wise to undertake.
Knowing that under the ruling system he
could at his pleasure change from a state

of peace to one of war, or the reverse, his
natural appetite for bloody deeds was
greatly sharpened. Furthermore, it happened that the deep wrongs to which he
was constantly subjected by the whites
increased in about the same ratio as his
power to avenge them. These are some of
the facts relating to the bands of Sioux
which hovered around Forts Phil. Kearney
and C. F. Smith in 1866. The troops were
not only far away from support and few
in numbers, but the infantry was not then
armed with breech-loading rifles.

It frequently happens on the plains that
wood and water cannot be found close together in the region where a post is to
be established. The wood for Fort Phil.
Kearney had to be cut and hauled to the
site on the river, a distance of some four
and a half miles. The duty required of
the troops was laborious and perilous in
the extreme. One portion of them was in
the woods cutting timber to house themselves in a terrible winter climate, another
portion was receiving and hauling, another

still was building at the fort, while the
fourth portion was charged with the difficult task of protecting the other three
from a savage foe, numerous, well armed,
brave, cunning, and hostile, but yet pro-
fessing peace.

In the forenoon of the 21st of December,
1866, a signal of danger was given to the
post by the picket guard on Sullivant's
Hill, about a mile and a half away ; and it
was soon ascertained that the wagon-train,
still further off on its way to the pinery
where the timber was cut, had halted and
formed into a defensive position against
Indians. A few shots were heard, and
Indians were seen passing to and fro
among the bushes which skirted the creek
in the distance. Orders were at once
issued for the available troops to start
to the rescue. Brevet Lieutenant-Colonel
Fetterman, though not designated by the
commander of the post, claimed the right
to command the detached force by virtue
of his rank, which was conceded, and he
accordingly took command. As Colonel

Fetterman's bravery and dash in the face
of danger were conspicuous, he was warned previous to starting to be careful, as
the Indians in the vicinity were known to
be brave, skilful, and cunning. He was
directed to "support the wood-train, relieve it, and return to the post." As the
command started out Indians reappeared
in clusters of four or five near the creek
and in the brush. They were carefully
watching the fort with a view to cut off
any small party that might move out.
A case-shot from the guns of the fort was
neatly plumped amongst them, when they
scattered and broke for the hills. Fetterman's command moved rapidly on and
passed out of sight. Soon the picket on
Sullivant's Hill reported that the wood-
train had broken corral and moved on to
the pinery, but nothing was heard from
Fetterman's detachment. About noon firing was heard in the distance. Soon it
became rapid, and the commandant of the
post, Colonel Carrington, immediately
called his working parties to arms and

started out all of his remaining force and two wagons, giving orders to join Colonel Fetterman at all hazards. The party proceeded swiftly to a ridge overlooking the supposed scene of action, but just as it reached there the firing ceased. Nothing was seen of Fetterman's party, but the fatal valley beyond was swarming with excited warriors, who challenged the soldiers to come down. The troops knew they had reached the ground from which sounds of Fetterman's guns had come, but not a man or horse of his command could be seen. As they moved cautiously forward to the spot the Indian skirmishers withdrew from the valley, and there were found eighty-one bodies weltering in their blood, amongst them Fetterman's and Brown's. It seemed to be the purpose of the Indians to permit this handful of troops to advance only far enough to see how completely and savagely their companions in arms had been butchered. No sooner had they taken a full view of the horrible field than the Indians in front, too numerous to cope with, advanced in force and drove the troops back slowly to the fort. At the close of this bloody day the longest of winter nights closed in upon this most desolate region, with one part of the isolated little garrison exhausted within and the other part lying dead without its enclosure. The next morning Colonel Carrington with eighty men moved out to make further developments as to the enemy and the fate of his party. Without opposition he soon reached the field of disaster and death. The road on the ridge where the final stand had evidently been made was strewn with arrows, arrowheads, scalp-poles, and broken heads of spears. There was abundant evidence that Colonel Fetterman and his little band had been surrounded by overwhelming numbers and cut off while in retreat. The details were left to conjecture, as not a single man lived to tell the tale. A few bodies were found at the north end of the divide, but most of them were heaped beside four rocks at the point nearest the fort, in a space about six feet square, that having apparently been the last refuge. Fetterman and Brown had each a revolver-shot in the left temple, and it was surmised that, in pursuance of an oft-repeated resolve, these two brave men, finding all hope gone, had died each by the other's hand rather than undergo the horrible tortures and lingering death to which they knew they would be subjected by their savage captors. All the signs of desperate resistance were there; but, alas! it was evident that no amount of valor could have saved them. Pools of blood on the roads and sides of the adjacent slopes showed where the Indians had bled, fatally no doubt; but they left no bodies. Two citizens happened to be in the garrison armed with "Henry rifles." This well-known repeater was at that time a novelty on the plains. So formidable was the weapon that these two men felt "invincible," as Colonel Carrington expresses it. They went out as volunteers with Colonel Fetterman, and appear to have taken, apart from the troops, a position in which they fought and died together. Their bodies were surrounded by the cartridge-shells which had fallen from their trusty rifles. The revenge visited upon their remains by the savages told how destructive their fire had been. One of the naked bodies contained as many as a hundred and five arrows.*

The mutilations inflicted by the Indians upon the heroic victims of this sad affair were horrible to a degree seldom known even in such atrocities. Eyes torn out and laid on the rocks ; noses, ears, chins, hands, feet cut off ; teeth chopped out ; every possible form of mutilation and torture that could be imagined by savages who have a genius for inventions of that description was practised. The bodies were gathered together by their companions and buried where they fell. Thus perished gallant men in the prime of life, full of vigor and of hope. While records,

---

* This shooting of arrows into the body is mostly done by boys after the battle has ended and the bodies have been stripped.

medals, monuments, and memory last
their services and sad fate will not be
forgotten by their country.

"Forty Degrees below Zero."

"O my son !
The ostentatious virtues which still press
For notice and for praise ; the brilliant deeds
Which live but in the eyes of observation—
These have their meed at once ; but there's a joy
To the fond votaries of fame unknown :
To hear the still, small voice of conscience speak
Its whispering plaudits to the silent soul."

THERE are countries whose soldiers lead lives of wild excitement and adventure during the short period of war, and of safety, indolence, and monotony through the long years of peace. We are always at war with "bad" Indians, and as the dead Indian is said to be the only *good* one, there is no prospect of early peace and safety for our troops. The ordinary duties in the far West, though without glory, are attended with dangers and sufferings no less terrible and

118

trying than those of the great wars, whose victims receive the unstinted sympathy of their fellow-men, and whose heroes are held up for ever to the admiring gaze of millions. The savage foe, the sudden storm, the pitiless wind, the biting frost, to be encountered every year by the soldier in the far West, call for an aggregate of courage, skill, and fortitude which grand battles do not demand.

It is something of a paradox that, while our troops are on the frontier to protect the civilized from the savage race, some of the most hazardous and arduous enterprises of the army have been against our own people. This sometimes grows out of using the army as an instrument for enforcing treaties made by the Government with the Indians; such, for example, as the treaty by which the Indians were assured that no white men should go into the "Black Hills country."

It was ascertained in the fall of 1874 that miners, tempted to the Black Hills by reports of gold deposits in that region, had made their arrangements to winter there, and it was resolved by the Government to remove them, using force if necessary.   While the Christian world was enjoying the festivities and pleasures of Christmas, 1874, the little band of soldiers at Red Cloud Agency, Dakota, was making hasty preparations for the arduous duty assigned to it.   The expedition consisted of one company of cavalry and a lieutenant and fifteen men of infantry, the whole under command of Brevet-Colonel Guy V. Henry, Captain Third United States Cavalry.

The weather was bitter cold.   The Indian was not to be feared.   He had left the war-path, and, retreating before the common enemy, had found shelter for the season in deep and secret cañons.   The pale-face alone was called upon to face the winter storms, and that in pursuit of his own people.   Leaving his Christmas dinner behind, he moved promptly and cheerfully.   The trail was plain down the White River to Spotted-Tail Agen-

cy, where "Falling Star," a noted Indian
guide, was to join and thenceforward conduct the party. But the thermometer was
now below zero, and "Falling Star," with
that discretion which is said to be the better part of valor, declined the honor and
clung to his camp-fire. A substitute was
found in a trapper who had been a soldier
some twenty years before, and who joined
in response to the impress of his early
training. Following White River to
Mounted Knee Creek, the expedition
struck out into the "Mauvais Terres," or
Bad Lands, a region which, without in-
tending profanity, has been likened to the
hilly parts of hell with the fires put out.

Ash Springs, midway between White
River and South Cheyenne, were reached
on New Year's eve. There was already
much suffering from cold, many being
frost-bitten. The thermometer registered
40° below zero, and the lee of the hills
afforded the only protection to be found
for the night. The next day the com
mand reached its destination, Elk Creek,

on which the offending miners were to
have been found ; but they were not there.
(It was afterwards discovered that they
had entered the forbidden lands from
quite an opposite direction.) After a thorough and fruitless search the return march
was taken up.   The suffering from the intense cold was now aggravated by a piercing wind.   It fortunately came on their
backs.   A little cover was found the last
night of the return march by camping on
the frozen surface of a small lake fringed
with brush.   The next day the wind
changed to their front and the driving
grains of ice beat in their faces.   Freezing and starving, men and horses toiled
on step by step, the soldiers of most endurance and strength arousing and drag-
ging the weaker ones, who, from time to
time, showed that they were falling into
freezing drowsiness and languor.   Fa-
tigued, almost worn out, to halt was
certain death. The only hope of safety
lay in struggling on. Many no longer felt
the cold. The painful, stinging bite of

the frost had been succeeded by the more solid freezing which drives the blood rapidly to the centre and produces that warm, delightful, drowsy sensation, the forerunner of danger and death.

With indomitable courage and resolution, and with unerring judgment, the officers and the sergeants seized in time the most dangerous cases and lashed them to their saddles, so that they might not fall asleep by the wayside. The situation was desperate, almost hopeless. Shelter was known to be not far away ; but human nature was exhausted, and the mind at last became as powerless to plan as the body was to execute. The only hope of safety was in the instinct and endurance of the horses. The order to "gallop" was given ; where, the commander himself hardly knew ; but the faithful animals, with their stiffened riders, went straight into the eye of the relentless storm at the best pace they could, and stopped only when they reached what seemed to be the gate of Paradise—a ranche inhabited by a white

man and a squaw, a blazing fire within
and a pile of wood without. The helpless
were quickly and carefully removed from
their saddles. The horses were corralled,
and then began that horrible process of
thawing out. Hands, feet, cheeks, ears,
noses, and, in some cases, other extremi-
ties were badly frozen. Snow and kero-
sene were the only remedies at hand for
the frozen parts. The cold was still so
intense that the owners of the ranche considered it a risk to go out for wood, and it
was with difficulty that freezing was prevented among the large party after they
were all under cover.

The post was not far distant, and in due
time wagons were sent to haul the sufferers back to their stations. Weeks and
months of agony and helplessness followed ; many, in fact, can never be well
again. The nervous system was in some
cases shocked beyond recovery. Finger
and toe nails dropped off, and the frozen
flesh decayed and sloughed away, exposing the bones. Some of Colonel Henry's

fingers were amputated, and for two months he was unable to make any use of his hands—having to be fed, dressed, etc.—and fifteen months after the occurrence his fingers had not all healed.

It has been the purpose in the foregoing account to give simply a general recital of facts, and not to point cases of special heroism or sacrifice, of which there doubtless were many. The consciousness of duty done according to orders is the reward alike of all the party, from the highest to the lowest.

One of the ablest, most interesting and instructive of recent publications, Colonel Dodge's work called "The Plains of the Far West," speaking of this expedition, says: "The recent sufferings of a command sent into the Black Hills are fresh in the minds of all. It is easy, seated in a comfortable office, to give orders for a winter campaign or movement of troops on the plains; but it usually means death to somebody. This is, of course, a part of the soldier's bargain, and it is the pride of our soldiers to obey orders, whether they lead to death by the cold of a plains storm or by the heat of the Indian stake. But such men deserve that there shall always be a necessity."

"Bison."

" Man's a strange animal and makes
Strange use of his own nature."
                                —BYRON.

WHEN the country was startled in 1876 by the exploits of "Sitting Bull," many wild rumors about the education of that distinguished Indian chief were set afloat ; one of them made him a graduate of the United States Military Academy. It is quite possible the story resulted from confounding "Bull" with "Bison."

A young man from Western Missouri reported as a cadet at West Point in 1844. His character, as it rapidly developed, harmonized with his personal appearance, and, taken together, they suggested for him the appropriate nickname of "Bison." He was a full-grown man, having a large

head covered with bushy, uncombed hair;
a square face; low, rectangular forehead;
small, deep-set, piercing eyes; straight,
short nose and heavy jaw; a bull neck
rising out of broad and massive shoulders; a long body tapering downward to
the hips, and short, stout arms and legs.
He was as suggestive of the American bison
as a man could be. As uncultivated as he
was uncouth, he was yet gifted with more
than ordinary talent, and not only passed
the examination for admission as a cadet,
but remained at the Academy the entire
term of four years, and mastered every
course of instruction. In character, however, he was from first to last a wild animal. Tamed a little by the restraint of
the Academy and the manifest advantages which were open to him, the reck-
less strain in his blood, breaking forth
from time to time, subjected him to frequent punishments and kept him on the
verge of dismissal. As a penalty for as-
saulting a superior officer, he was deprived of the furlough given to his classmates

at the end of their second year. This loss
of two months' coveted liberty was a peculiarly severe punishment and made him
more desperate.

Destitute of personal fear and under no
moral restraint, his animal passions were
curbed only to escape detection and dismissal. He became a terror to the neighboring village, which he visited by stealth
with a cunning that seemed more than
human. Careful matrons learned to bar
their doors against him, and, like the
clucking hens, gathered their broods beneath their wings at his approach. Despite all precaution, however, while still
a cadet he succeeded in entrapping a
young woman to ruin through a mock
marriage, and this without discovery until
long after he had left her and West Point.
At the graduating examination, although
proficient in the various branches of instruction, his sins were heavier than he
could bear. He was pronounced deficient
in conduct, denied a diploma, and dis-
missed from the service.

A year or two after this the city of Galveston, Texas, was aroused by the discovery that a law student had, under promise of marriage, shamefully deceived and wronged a young lady of most respectable family. Her uncle, pistol in hand, found the student in his office, and demanded immediate signature to a paper already prepared and a prompt fulfilment of the marriage vows. The student calmed the outraged uncle, promised everything, unlocked his desk for a pen with which to sign, but quickly brought out a revolver instead, and, holding it at the uncle's head, drove him with jeers and curses from the room. This was the end of "Bison's" law studies. He knew Texas too well to wait the appearance of Judge Lynch, and fled on the instant, finding safety among the Indians and outlaws on the northern frontier of the State. It is probably through this part of his history that he has been confounded with "Sitting Bull." How long he remained with the Indians, or what he did, is not

fully known; but incidents have come to
light showing that the devil within him
would not be controlled, and that he
"fell upon whate'er was offered, like a
priest, a shark, an alderman, or pike."

While one of the Pacific Mail steam-
ships was making her regular voyage from
Panama to San Francisco, having touched
at Acapulco, a strange man all of a sudden appeared on deck. When questioned
he would not tell when, where, or under
what circumstances he got aboard, but
claimed to be an officer of the army, and
tried to identify himself in that character.
This failed, and, having no money, he was
called upon to work his passage. He
flatly refused, and defied the captain
when he undertook to enforce his orders.
A fight ensued, in which the entire ship's
crew was on one side and "Bison" alone
on the other. The match for a time did
not seem unequal, but was finally settled
by one of the sailors, armed with a hand-
spike, getting behind and felling "Bison"
to the deck by a blow on the head.

Stunned and bleeding, he was still so dangerous that they put him in irons; and when the ship ran near the shore along the coast of Lower California, his shackles were removed and he was sent off in a small boat to be cast adrift in a desolate region, friendless, penniless, breadless. He would not wait to be landed. When within two or three hundred yards of the shore he sprang from the boat and swam away to land. His next appearance was as a herder on one of the large stock ranches in southern California, where he soon engaged the affections of the owner's daughter. The father, however, it seems, discovered the affair in time and ran the "Bison" off, and he made his way to San Francisco, at that time the paradise of men of his stamp. Friendless and homeless, he found shelter in the narrow space, not wide enough for an alley, between the walls of two houses. This he in time boarded over and converted into a den, and, strange to say, he found a companion to share it with him.

Muscle, of which he had plenty, made gold in those days, and working on the wharves, piling lumber, etc., paid well enough. He was soon pre-eminent among the vicious characters then abounding in California. His talent and education added to his capacity as a leader in vice ; and his influence and acquaintance were not limited to San Francisco, but soon extended among his class over the State, and he was said to have been a member of Jauquin's band of robbers. About this time he began a desperate struggle with the most dangerous of foes. Heretofore he had only sparred pleasantly with King Alcohol. Now they stripped off the gloves and began in earnest. After drinking all of one evening with a companion the two left the saloon together. His companion was soon after found in a dark alley, murdered, and "Bison" fled.

Arizona was at that time one of the most remote, unattractive, and unfrequented regions in the United States. The few troops there watching and pursuing the Apaches were largely dependent for success upon their guides. "Bison" offered himself in this capacity. Although he had seen but little of the country, he possessed in a remarkable degree that instinct which is the principal element in the character of a guide. His career in this field was, as usual, one of adventure and danger, and finally ended in death from disease, or, as some believed (from supposed treachery), at the hands of the Apaches, whom he had joined as a friend. Adapting a fugitive couplet:

> " Washington, Bison, Bull, and St. Paul,
> God in his wisdom created them all."

"Outnumbered but not Outdone."

"A charming picture. It is good
To look upon a chief like this,
In whom the spirit moulds the form,
Where favoring nature, oft remiss,
With eagle mien expressive, has endued
A man to kindle strains that warm."

THE two years of Fort Phil. Kearney's existence — from July 13, 1866, to July 31, 1868 — were passed by its garrison in a fight for life. The post was in the heart of the enemy's country. The savages were well armed and could feed on the buffalo, to be found in great abundance. The odds were vastly in their favor, and, emboldened by success, especially the defeat and total destruction of Fetterman's command * in the open field, they at times seemed to be on the eve of annihilating our entire force. But

* See " The Fatal Valley," pages 101 to 116

135

with courage, vigilance, and industry, the
troops struggled on from day to day,
fighting the foe, and cutting and hauling
timber from the pinery, four or five miles
away, to build up the post and supply
wood for use as fuel. The choppers
worked under cover of a surrounding line
of skirmishers, and every wagon-train
made its weary trip to and fro protected
by flankers and an advance and rear
guard. The Indians were at home, and,
being very numerous, could go and come,
threaten, attack, and retire, as suited their
convenience. This was in a time of so-
called peace. The condition of affairs,
which imposed heavy labor and exhaust-
ing watchfulness on the troops, afforded
the savages the most agreeable pastime.
A year of this existence, from July, 1866,
to July, 1867, had passed away. That the
troops, but few in number, were confined
to the defensive was as well understood
by the Indians as by the whites. Perhaps
this knowledge served to make the former
over-confident, and to prepare them for a

lesson they were soon to receive. They either did not know or did not appreciate the fact that, since their complete victory over Fetterman, six months before, the infantry had been armed with breech-loaders, the full effect of which weapon in savage warfare was then unknown.

In the latter part of July, 1867, Captain James Powell, First Lieutenant John C. Jenness, and Company "C," of the Twenty-seventh United States Infantry, were assigned to the duty of guarding the choppers in the pinery. The service was important and hazardous, and was well calculated to test a commander's readiness and fertility in resource, as well as to try his courage and vigilance. Captain Powell found the choppers working in two parties, nearly a mile apart, each with a train of ox-teams in attendance to haul the timber and wood to the fort. The problem was to protect the choppers while at work and the cattle when grazing, and to guard the trains until they came under cover of the fort. The captain at once made his

dispositions. Every man—guards, choppers, drivers, herders, etc.—was told exactly where to go and what to do in case
of attack. The wagons were arranged so
as to form an irregular circular enclosure,
or "*corral*," for defence. The wagon-
bodies, fourteen in number, with loop-
holes cut in the sides, were taken from the
running gear and placed bottom down on
the circumference of the circle. The intervals between the ends of the wagon-beds
were filled with yokes, tents, grain-sacks,
and other things at hand. Two wagons,
one loaded with provisions and the other
with clothing, were placed on the outside
of the enclosure at the weakest points, to
give additional strength where most needed. The mountain rose abruptly from the
pinery, and its rocky side, within plain
view of the corral, afforded excellent defensive positions. These were carefully
selected, and the choppers themselves, and
the guard immediately on duty, instructed
in the use of them, and told to fly there
and fight to the last in case of a serious

attack. The captain, a lieutenant, twenty-
five soldiers, and five frontiersmen acting
as guides, interpreters, etc., held the corral and looked after the general welfare.
The first effort of the Indians in making
an attack, especially the mounted tribes,
is almost invariably to *stampede* the enemy's animals. The temptation to this
course seems to be so great that it may be
looked upon as their regular opening. If
successful it strengthens them in subsequent operations, as the white man is
at great disadvantage on the vast plains
without beasts of burden. This movement is generally effected without loss ;
and, if it fails as an attack, it is very
likely to pay as a robbery. Stealing animals is not only of substantial importance
to the Indians, but plunder and glory are
nearly synonymous terms in their vocabu-
lary. It is generally the case, therefore,
that the first note of alarm comes from the
herders or the pickets in advance of them,
and in time for preparation. In this respect the irresistible thieving propensity

of the noble red-man works to our advantage. For three or four days after Captain Powell had established himself everything was quiet and peaceful. Nothing but the noise and stir of his own party disturbed the solitude of the boundless region, in which they seemed to be alone. The dull routine of camp went on day and night without an incident to break the monotony. But never for a moment did the sagacious commander relax in vigilance or readiness. The earliest dawn of those long summer days found his watchful sentinels peering with well-trained eyes into the gray distance for the stealthy movements of the dusky savage. Early in the morning of the 2d of August some half-bent forms were faintly seen by the sentinels over the herd, gliding like spectres along the ravines in the distance. The surprise had already failed. The different parts of the force quietly but promptly assumed their prearranged positions and duties. Hardly had they done so when small bodies of mounted Indians

—the stampeding parties—about sixty in
the aggregate, were observed emerging
from the ravines some six hundred yards
from the corral. Making a charge upon
the corral as a feint, they tried to scatter
and drive off the herd grazing near the
pinery ; but the danger had been signalled
to all the outlying parties, and the attempt was not only foiled but the Indians
were evidently surprised at their reception, and, without a casualty among the
troops, retreated with severe loss.   As
soon as this preliminary operation for
seizing the herd was well under way, the
savages from another quarter attacked the
choppers and their guards, who had taken
their positions among the rocks.   The
herders, who had repulsed the assault
upon themselves, rushed to the assistance
of their imperilled companions, and Captain Powell, leaving his corral for the moment, deployed his men and covered the
movement of the herders until they had
safely joined the guards on the mountain
side.   Four of the soldiers were killed

during this movement. The location of
the corral and the positions of the troops
among the rocks were wisely chosen, and
a rapid and well-directed fire upon the
Indians, exposed and mounted as they
were, soon drove them off with heavy loss.
But they were only repulsed, not defeated. The corral was now to bear the brunt
of their fury. Five hundred chosen warriors of the Cheyennes and Arapahoes
mounted and formed for the assault. The
captain distributed his men about the enclosure, lying down, as far as practicable, in the wagon-beds, which sat on the
ground, and covered them with blankets,
etc., from the wagon load of clothing
which had been brought out for issue.
Then they waited for the charge of the
five hundred, which was repulsed more
promptly and effectually than the most
confident had even dared to hope it
would be. But this seemed to be only
the effort of the enemy's forlorn hope,
intended to draw the fire of the troops
and make them spend their ammunition.

The real attack was in preparation. The warriors for it were seen in the distance, three thousand in number, swarming over the hills and valleys, and finding their places in the wild and desperate cavalcade. Captain Powell made the most of the little time left him before the impending crash. More blankets and clothing were quickly snatched from the wagon in which they were loaded, and were stuffed into the openings in the ingenious parapet, and were placed in thick folds to protect the men as they lay in the wagon-beds. All of the weapons and tools, guns, pistols, axes, hatchets, hammers, spades, etc., which could in any emergency be used for offence or defence, were promptly distributed among the men. But few words were spoken, yet all felt that every man in the corral had made a resolve, more binding than any oath, to fight to the last.

The unuttered pledge was well kept. The column of attack, some fifteen hundred mounted warriors, advancing with wild yells, charged at full speed upon the

little band behind the rude intrenchment.
The dauntless few were ready. A most
destructive fire was opened as soon as the
column was within easy range, and was
kept up with a rapidity and accuracy absolutely appalling to the foe. He staggered, stopped, and fell back in confusion.
But not realizing the power of the breech-
loader when amply supplied with ammunition, the column reformed and renewed
the charge within two or three minutes,
only, however, to meet with a more disastrous repulse.

Then, broken and dispirited, but gath-
ering up and carrying their dead, they
sought shelter in the timber. The expe-
riment of riding their ponies over the
breastworks had failed.

Their next move was to advance about
fifty sharpshooters armed with rifles taken
from the troops in the Fetterman massacre. These crawled up the ravines,
holding before them bunches of grass like
gabions; but they found more than their
match in this species of warfare. The men

in the wagon-beds saw through the thin
disguise and rapidly picked them off.
While this was going on, the main body
of the Indians had dismounted, left their
horses in the woods, and to the number of
two thousand, led by a nephew of the
famous Red Cloud, advanced to the attack
on foot and entirely naked. Their close
line, in the shape of a horse-shoe, came
forward at a walk to within five hundred
yards of the corral; then, taking up a
slow run, they came within ten paces of
the stronghold before they yielded to the
volleys which were poured into them.
Baffled and dismayed, again they turned
and fled, their leader and many of his followers having fallen dead upon the field.
Their fire, though rapid, had generally
passed over the beleaguered party and
had done but little harm. Lieutenant
Jenness, however, and one private, who
had risen up in the corral, notwithstanding repeated injunctions, and thus need-
lessly though gallantly exposed themselves to the enemy's fire, had been killed.

The despondent savages had gone far out of range to hold a "talk." A new form of attack was the result. About three hundred of them had formed into detachments of eight or ten each, and advanced at intervals of about twenty paces, uttering a weird and curious chant. The first volley, fired when they were within two hundred yards of the corral, checked and dispersed them. This was evidently a feint. The real attack came from the opposite and an entirely new direction. Fortunately, it was discovered in time. The Indians engaged in it sprang from the ground as if by magic and rushed desperately forward. But there was no lack of vigilance, readiness, skill, courage, and ammunition in the charmed circle.

The cunningly-conceived and daringly-executed assault was met and repelled as all of the preceding ones had been. An interval of fifteen or twenty minutes followed, during which the Indians were heard chanting in the distance. They were making "good medicine" for a final

effort. Taking advantage of their great
numbers, they organized an assault by detached columns, advancing simultaneously
from all directions. But these various
modifications in the mode of attack produced no change in the character and
vigor of the defence. The besieged, cool
and confident, clung to their intrenchments, rifles in hand, and with eyes fixed
upon the approaching foe. The aim was
unerring, and the fire, though distributed
around the circle, was rapid and merciless. The determined savages struggled
forward against it until they were within
fifty paces of the enclosure, when one of
the parties faltered and broke, and the
others quickly retired.

During the entire fight well-posted Indians, apparently assigned especially to
that duty, had kept up a continuous fire
of burning arrows upon the corral. They
totally failed to start a blaze, and there
was nothing explosive to reach ; but the
charred arrows found embedded in the
piles of clothing and sticking in the

wagon-bodies after the struggle had ended
showed how nearly successful these dangerous efforts had been.

But the agony was nearly over. Succor
was at hand. Like the loud slogan of the
Campbells at the memorable siege of
Lucknow, the sound of a field-piece came
floating on the air from the direction of
the Fort. Its meaning was promptly interpreted by besiegers and besieged. The
undaunted little band in the corral were
about to spring to their feet when the
wary captain bade them lie still, but to
respond at once to the welcome signal by
a ringing cheer. The "three times three"
which they sent forth can only issue from
throats of men to whom relief comes after
long hours of silent death-struggles with
their fellow-men. Their cheers, piercing
with terror the hearts of the savage
hordes, travelled gladly on until they answered the greeting of the loud cannon.
The Indians, so often beaten back and dis-
couraged, were completely demoralized by
the appearance of this new danger. Hur-

rying away their dead and wounded, they hastily withdrew, and thus terminated one of the most desperate conflicts which has ever occurred between the white man and the savage. The latter greatly outnumbered the former, the relative strength of the contending forces being about as a hundred to one. There was skill as well as bravery on both sides. The advantages of the whites—beyond the *morale* due to civilization and higher intelligence— arose from their perfect coolness, their breech-loading arms, and their intrenchments. It is one of the anomalies in Indian character, generally speaking, that while these people instinctively seize every natural feature which will afford cover in a field of battle, they have not the least aptitude either in constructing or attacking artificial defences. A fight in which there is no chance to run away is neither attractive nor honorable in their sight. They have often tried to draw our troops from their breastworks by taunts of cowardice and challenges to the open field.

In his official report, made soon after this fight, Captain Powell gave the Indian loss at sixty killed and a hundred severely wounded; but this estimate was much too low. The facts which have since come to light have enabled the captain and the frontiersmen who were with him to present more accurate figures, showing that there were about three hundred killed and as many wounded. The troops lost Lieutenant Jenness and five enlisted men killed and two enlisted men wounded.

In the official order publishing the details of this fight the conduct of the troops was pleasingly referred to. The department commander said: "Major Powell, by his coolness and firmness in this most creditable affair, has shown what a few determined men can effect with good arms and strong hearts, even with such temporary defensive arrangements as are almost always at hand, and that it is always safer, leaving out the questions of duty and professional honor, to stand and fight Indians than to retreat from them."

Of Lieutenant Jenness it was recorded that he "fell while affording to his men a fine example of coolness and daring."

This occurrence, although a crushing defeat to the Indians, no doubt contributed to the accomplishment of their purpose of forcing our withdrawal from Forts Phil. Kearney and C. F. Smith. Both these posts were abandoned at the end of the following July, and the natives were left masters of vast regions over which our troops have since been compelled to make arduous and bloody campaigns.

The principal actor in the heroic defence above recounted deserves more than a passing notice, and we feel our task would be incomplete were we to close without adverting to him. Captain Powell entered the army as a private soldier prior to the opening of our late civil war. Soon after the commencement of the war, being then a sergeant of the First Dragoons, he was appointed a second lieutenant in the Eighteenth Infantry, was promoted first lieutenant in 1861 and captain in 1864,

and in 1868 was placed upon the retired
list of the army, being incapacitated for
active service, the result of gun-shot
wounds received at the battle of Jonesboro, Georgia, on the 1st of September,
1864. He received the brevet of captain
in 1863 for gallant and meritorious services during the Atlanta campaign and
at the battle of Jonesboro, Georgia; was
brevetted a major September 1, 1864, for
gallant services at Chickamauga, and
lieutenant-colonel August 2, 1867, for gallant conduct in fight with Indians on that
date near Fort Phil. Kearney. This last
brevet was the reward for the bravery and
endurance recounted in the foregoing narrative. It is a remarkable illustration of
the courage and endurance of this brave
soldier that, while he was fighting against
overwhelming numbers of savage Indians
on the 2d of August, 1867, he was then a
sufferer from wounds received in battle in
September, 1864, and which ultimately
necessitated his retirement from the career
he loved so well. Honor to whom honor

is due. Our hero's comrades fully and cheerfully bear tribute to his deeds of heroism, and point to him as a living example of what can be achieved by the soldier of steadfast qualities and courage.

"Bill and Dan."

MANY strange incidents come under
the observation of our army officers
while serving on the Western frontiers. The monotony of garrison life is
often relieved by the appearance at the
post of natives or pilgrims to the far
West. The agreeable variety generally
receives a warm welcome, and questions
eagerly pass from one to another as to
what is taking place in each one's world.
The following incidents are gleaned from
the sources referred to.

Bill and Dan were whole-souled, industrious, sensible brothers, devoted to each
other with more than ordinary affection.
Their early lives had been one continued
struggle for daily bread. With strong
common sense, they had no education, not
being able even to read or write. Like

154

many others, finding no chance of success in their native town, they started with an ox-team to the land of gold—California. In due time they reached their destination, and soon their sterling qualities and perseverance bore golden fruit. Slowly but surely their "pile" grew larger, and when it amounted to about a hundred thousand dollars they began to find it necessary to have some one who could keep their accounts, having so far attended to such matters themselves in a hap-hazard sort of a way. They cast about for a suitable partner, and, having found what they deemed the right man, he was admitted into the firm. The new partner was not only an educated man but smart and dishonest. The confidence which secured his admission soon ripened into implicit faith, and the whole business fell under his administration. This traitor and thief falsified the accounts, and, by abuse of signatures to blanks entrusted to him, swindled the unfortunate brothers out of the larger part of their hard-earned

savings, and then absconded. This so
thoroughly disgusted Bill and Dan with
both education and "business" that, taking what money remained to them, they
devoted themselves exclusively to the care
of their cattle and sheep in Oregon, per-
sistently declining all assistance and all
companions, except a faithful and devoted
Indian boy some fourteen years of age.
Soon this life of exclusion and monotony
became wearisome, and, in a desire for
change, the brothers gathered together
their flocks and herds—eighteen hundred
sheep, some cattle and mules, and a few
horses—and, carrying with them all their
money (about sixty-two hundred dollars
in twenty-dollar gold-pieces), they started
for California, driving their herds before
them, and accompanied only by the Indian boy. Finding no suitable abiding-
place, they continued their journey to the
south and east until they entered the
deserts of Arizona. There the lack of
water and grass, with the hardships incident to their long march, rendered help

necessary in the care of the stock. They
deliberated for a long time as to whether
they should hire some one to assist them,
and, with many misgivings, finally resolved to trust once more and take a
new hand. He came to them well recommended, but, alas! turned out a counter-
part of their first venture in the way of
partnership, and before getting out of the
Territory he succeeded in stealing and
escaping with all their gold. Much time
was spent in fruitless efforts to capture
him, but without success. However, long
after they had abandoned the pursuit and
resumed their wanderings the rascal was
taken by the civil authorities, but, strange
to say, was released, having secured cle-
mency, perhaps, by dividing the stolen
money. But, as if by the special inter-
vention of a higher power, he was not permitted long to enjoy his ill-gotten gains.
He was soon after the occurrence killed
by some of his own kind in a drunken
brawl. Bill and Dan, however, recovered
nothing.

Henceforth the unfortunate pair
trusted only each other and the Indian
boy. Late in the summer of 1876 they
reached the Canadian River, in what is
known as the Pan-handle of Texas, a region frequented by bad characters. Here
the brothers pitched their tents. They
were quiet and fearless, injured no one, in
fact knew no one, and gave no cause for
offence. They had, it is true, an innate
feeling of dislike and contempt for Mexicans—"Greasers," as they are called—
which subsequent events suggest may
have unwittingly shown itself. They
lived simply and peaceably, taking turns
in watching their herds and in the neces
sary duties of the camp. They had jour-
neyed long to get away from the land
of their misfortunes, and congratulated
themselves that they had now secured a
haven of rest and left all enemies and
troubles behind. The Fates, however, had
willed it otherwise. One day, early in
the winter of 1876, when it was Dan's
turn in camp and Bill's out with the

stock, the latter was walking quietly
through the woods, unconscious of a foe
or danger ; a Mexican desperado, lurk-
ing in the bushes, slipped up behind
and shot him in the back, killing him
instantly. The wretch then turned towards the camp. On the way he met a
Mexican acquaintance, told him what he
had just done, and ordered *him* to go at
once to the camp and kill the other brother (Dan). Afraid to refuse, the poltroon
consented, but, before reaching his destination, turned away and went to a Mexican house in the vicinity frequented by
this class, and related what had occurred.
The desperado, suspecting that his villanous order would not be executed, went
himself to see to it. Dan and the boy,
sitting by the camp-fire, ignorant of the
bloody deed and wholly unsuspicious,
greeted the bravo kindly and invited
him to dismount. This he declined, but
asked the favor of a brand from the em-
bers to light his cigarette. Dan stooped
to get it, when the fiend shot him through

the back of the head and then deliberately murdered the boy. Having accomplished this, he rode with perfect coolness to the Mexican house and told the story of the triple murder. Among the men in the house was the one who had disobeyed his order. To escape discovery and the dreaded vengeance of the displeased monster, this man hid himself in the bed. But the villain's search finally disclosed the trembling victim, and, stripping off the covers, he drew his pistol to shoot the begging coward. But his villany now met its just reward. He had become too dangerous even for his own comrades. Just as he was about to fire his arm was knocked up by one of the bystanders, a knife was thrust into his ribs by another, and a blow with a chair from a third settled his fate. Now that the bully was on the defensive and at a disadvantage, the more timid rushed in and soon despatched him with their weapons.

Such was the tragic fate of two brave and faithful brothers. In their lives they

were true and constant to each other, and
in death they were not divided. Having
been such a short time in their new home,
no one had become much acquainted with
them. They were known only as Bill and
Dan to the few who had come across
them. Their flocks and herds, left without a shepherd, wandered far and near,
and it was a long time before any one
could ascertain even the names of their
ill-fated owners.

He Curses the Apache.

A SCOUTING party in the Rocky Mountains observed a mounted squaw in the distance. The papoose on her back was as motionless as the woman and pony, all appearing to be in a doze. But this was a shrewd and watchful sentinel, and, without apparent motion or sound, she reported to others the presence of strangers. A horseman was soon seen passing through the woods, and, striking the trail in front, came galloping back, called a halt, and introduced himself as Colonel Pfeiffer, an old soldier, frontiersman, and guide. The friendly Indians among whom he lived had kept him for weeks fully informed of the movements of the scouting party, and had even given him the name and rank of the officer in charge. His appearance was to offer wel-

come. He led the way to the cabin which
he had recently completed a few miles
deeper in the forest. Building a second
house is an event with the pioneer, and
the advantages of this one were pointed
out with evident pride and pleasure. Instead of having but a single room, this
modern structure consisted of "two pens
and a passage," with a roof over the
whole. The only tools used in constructing the house and making the furniture
for it were an axe, an auger, and a hand-
saw. The mud fireplace in the *corner* instead of the end of the kitchen showed
that the Mexican influence had been at
work, and it soon appeared that the wife,
whose murder is narrated further on, was
a native of New Mexico. Poles across the
passage as racks for saddles, robes, etc.,
benches for seats, a section of a large pine-
tree like a butcher's block as a table, with
a raised platform of poles, one end supported in the wall, as a bedstead, were
improvements which the colonel pointed
out as making his new residence far more

convenient than the old one. A bearskin, hanging at full length in the end of one room, covered a door leading into the storehouse, which contained sacks of flour on one side and sacks of beans on the other, with a few bags of salt—the supply for the year. The colonel remarked that he was a poor bread-maker, and, having had beans for thirty years, he was beginning to get tired of them, which he feared would soon deprive him of that variety in food which health requires. In fact, he already complained, and said if the guest had any pills he would be very thankful for a few doses. He did not seem to care what effect they were designed to produce. He simply wanted medicine. Fortunately for him, there were no pills. Pipes and tobacco, however, were furnished in lieu of pills. The veteran pioneer, as he smoked, related incidents in his adventurous life, most of which had long before formed the subjects of official reports to the Government. He was not only a fellow-frontiersman, but for a time a brother soldier, of the celebrated

Kit Carson. While they were stationed together once at Fort Garland, Colorado, Kit, as commanding officer, had made an order that no liquor should be sold. When he returned to the post after an absence of a couple of hours one afternoon, he found that Captain Pfeiffer had assumed command, issued an order permitting the sale of liquor temporarily, and that the sutler's stock of "pisen" had all been distributed, the temporary commander having bought a ten-gallon "cag" for himself. Kit rebuked his subordinate for assumption of authority. The latter only said in explanation that, having no copy of the Army Regulations, he had proceeded according to common sense, and it did seem to him right and reasonable to give the boys a chance at the liquor as soon as the responsibility rested on his shoulders; and that if his superior officer thought the order a bad one he had only to countermand it. The liquor had all been distributed.

One post was not large enough for two

such distinguished and determined characters. Captain Pfeiffer was sent to command Fort McRae, New Mexico. Years
of hardship and exposure, sleeping generally on the ground, and often in the rain
and snow, had produced rheumatic pains,
from which he was a constant sufferer.
Certain hot springs near the Fort had
frequently given him relief in early days,
and while in command he resolved to
try them again. The Apache Indians,
always treacherous and dangerous, were
at this time his deadliest foes. With a
guard of six chosen men, and accompanied by his wife, an Indian girl, and
a company laundress, the captain one
morning pitched his tent near the "Ojo
Caliente," or warm springs, only eight
miles distant from the Fort. A stealthy
body of Apaches had watched every
movement, but a thorough reconnoissance failed to discover any trace of an
enemy, and the party went into camp with
a feeling of security. In the afternoon the
three women strolled away together be-

yond the springs, and the captain went
into the bathing-pool, a hundred yards or
so from the tents, first taking the precaution to post two trusty sentinels to keep
watch while he was in the bath. Neglect-
ing the experience of a lifetime, he failed
to take his rifle with him. While in the
water he heard the crack of rifles, and
started up to see his two sentinels fall,
each shot through the head. The Apaches
had already captured the three women,
and were approaching, each woman being
pushed along as a shield in front of an
Indian. Naked as he was, the captain,
wounded as he ran, flew to his tent and
seized his rifle. The camp was surprised,
and, being sharply fired upon by the enemy, was demoralized. The leader alone,
calm and desperate, faced the savage foe.
Calling aloud in English to his wife, who
was held in front of the chief, to fall to
the ground, he lodged a bullet in the Indian's brain as she did so. Then, hoping
to gain and cross the river, which was
near, and thus improve his chances for

combat and escape, he turned to flee, when he was pierced through the side with an arrow. Continuing his flight, he was pursued only by a single Indian. The others, probably thinking his wounds fatal, did not doubt that the one savage could destroy him, and so went hastily to plundering the camp. Weakened by the loss of blood, the fugitive was overtaken. Turning suddenly, he grappled the pursuer, threw him to the ground, and, in the death-struggle which ensued, succeeded in wrenching a knife from the savage's hand and despatching him with it. The river was crossed; the naked, bleeding, and half-crazed victim continued his flight, lacerated by thorns and stones, until he fell fainting in the brush. The direful news was carried to the Fort by those who escaped. There was mounting in hot haste, and a rapid pursuit. The savages were twenty miles away before the cavalrymen drew near them. Then, finding they could not make good their escape with the plunder and the prisoners, the fiends resolved to shoot and abandon the latter. The bodies of the three women, pierced by bullets, were found, one after the other, on the trail of the fugitives. Life was not yet extinct. They were borne tenderly back to the Fort by the sorrowing troopers. The laundress alone recovered to tell the sad story. Tracked to the river by his blood, a search beyond revealed the wounded and fainting frontiersman, who lived to relate these events years after their occurrence, and to curse the Apaches. Old and alone in his cabin among the Utes, his existence appears a dreary one. But the hardy frontiersman has interests and pleasures of which the dwellers in cities know nothing. Privation and exposure are his pastime ; danger is merely a welcome excitement. To his indomitable energy and pluck, and to the services and sacrifices of our little army, do we owe the opening up of the vast Western territory with its countless treasures.

"A Man-Trap."

TREACHERY, whether natural or learned from the whites, seems now to be a fixed feature in the Indian's character. Even when receiving bounty from the hands of the Government he is very generally plotting the destruction of the agents entrusted with its distribution. The following is a striking evidence of this trait.

A large body of Sioux Indians, composed of the bands of Brulés, Ogalallas, and Minneconjoux, had been encamped for several days prior to the 19th of August, 1854, in the vicinity of Fort Laramie, Wyoming Territory, awaiting the arrival of the Indian agent charged with the distribution of their annuities. On the 18th of August an ox, belonging to some Mormon emigrants also encamped near Fort Lara-

mie, was stolen and killed by one of the
Indians. The owner of the ox complained of this transaction to the commander
of the fort, and almost at the same time
a Sioux leader, called "The Bear," chief
of the Brulé band, reported the occurrence to the commandant. He stated that
the offender was a Minneconjou, residing temporarily in the Brulé camp, and
suggested that a detachment of soldiers
be sent to the camp to demand his surrender, saying he had no doubt the demand would be readily complied with.
The suggestion was adopted, and on the
19th of August Brevet Second Lieutenant
John L. Grattan, Sixth United States Infantry, with a detachment of twenty-nine
men of Company G of that regiment,
riding in a wagon and armed as infantry,
but taking in addition a twelve-pounder
howitzer and a mountain howitzer drawn
by mules, was directed to bring in the
marauding Indian, being cautioned, however, not to incur unnecessary risk in so
doing.

To get to the Brulé camp it was necessary to pass the camps of the Ogalallas and Minneconjoux. As the troops neared the first camp Lieutenant Grattan, as a precautionary measure, directed his men to load their pieces, but not to cap them (these were the days of muzzle-loaders) ; and after proceeding a little further, when within a short distance of the Brulé camp, he halted his command and loaded his two pieces of artillery, to one of which he acted as gunner until he fell dead beside it. He then informed his men of the nature of the service required of them, and gave special instructions as to their conduct. On reaching the edge of the camp he sent for "The Bear," so as to avail himself of his authority and influence in securing the offender. A bitter feeling existed between the Indians and the interpreter who accompanied the troops, and unfortunately this important functionary was drunk and particularly offensive on this occasion. "The Bear" came in obedience to the summons, but in pursuance

of his plot, or aggravated by the threats of
the interpreter, and finding he could not
control his young men, he refused to de-
liver up the accused Minneconjou, telling Lieutenant Grattan that if he must
have him to go and take him. This challenge fixed the lieutenant's determination
not to be balked, and he resolved to take
the insulting chief at his word. It was a
significant circumstance that, although the
offender was a Minneconjou, his lodge
was not only in the Brulé camp, but was
adjoining "The Bear's" lodge in the centre of the encampment. The lieutenant
dismounted from his horse, and, taking his
position as gunner to the twelve-pounder
howitzer, led the way into the hostile
camp, the mountain howitzer and the
infantry following. Old Indian traders
whose stores were adjoining the camp
saw the trouble brewing, but were unable
to avert it or bring about an understanding between the whites and the Indians.
From the time the troops entered the
camp the young braves were seen to slip

out of their lodges with their guns, bows, and arrows, and conceal themselves in the surrounding bushes and below the bank of the river on which the camp was situated. There were not less than fifteen hundred warriors present, but the period was one of comparative peace, and the lieutenant proceeded, no doubt, upon the presumption that he had only to assert the vim and majesty of his Government for the arrest of an acknowledged offender; and so he went into something worse, if possible, than an ambuscade—it was a perfect man-trap.

The older Indians were clamorous for delay, thereby indicating either the difficulty they had in restraining their young men or the existence of a plot to give the warriors ample time to get ready. Lieutenant Grattan was undaunted, and determined to bring the matter to an immediate issue by submitting the alternative of an instant surrender of the Minneconjou or commencement of hostilities against the Brulés. Having presented his ultimatum, "The Bear," with whom he stood face to face, turned and walked sulkily away. The traders, who were observing the scene from the roof of the store hard by, heard the sharp sound of musketry and saw the flight of arrows, and then the heavy report of each howitzer came out upon the air. Lieutenant Grattan and part of his men were lying dead by the guns, and the remainder were trying to fight their way through the swarms of enraged savages, who surrounded and rushed upon them with knives in their hands. All of this was taken in at the first glance. In a minute or so more the last white man in the party had been slain, nearly all falling by arrows or knives. The single round fired by the troops had passed over the Indians, who were lying flat on the ground, the only effect being to inflict three wounds on "The Bear," and one each on two or three other Indians who happened to be exposed.

The Indians, glutted with blood and in-

toxicated with their success, plundered
the agent's store and the trading estab-
lishments; but the lives of the traders
were spared through the intercession of
some of the Indians with whom they were
connected by marriage. The savages then
resolved to attack the Fort, which they knew
to be much weakened by the slaughter of
Lieutenant Grattan's detachment and the
loss of the two howitzers, which had been
a great terror to the savages. The counsel
of the older warriors, however, prevailed,
and they abandoned their design, but immediately moved their camps across the
North Platte River, and then for two days
indulged in the general license which the
successful butchery permitted. Some of
the Indians proposed to kill the traders,
and thus destroy all the whites within
reach; but others, with rare friendliness
and gallantry, came to the rescue and
saved them at the risk of their own lives.

Another very unusual phase of Indian
character appeared. In wandering over
the battle-field an Indian, about twelve at

night, found the body of a soldier in which there was yet life. He raised and took the man to the trader's store, reaching there just as the dispute above mentioned was over. The unfriendly Indians proposed to kill the wounded soldier at once; but the Indian who had brought him in stood over his body and said: "If you kill this soldier you must kill me, for I shall die with him." It was, however, not safe for the poor victim to remain in the house, and his Indian friend escorted him for a mile and a half on the road to the Fort, some eight miles distant; but the poor sufferer, weak and bewildered, wandered back to the trading-house, which by an accession of hostile Indians was made more unsafe than when he left it. He was concealed in the bushes, from which he soon emerged again, and was then hidden in an old out-house until one of the white men mounted and, taking the soldier up behind, rode with him to the Fort. But these kind efforts only prolonged for a short time the life of

the last survivor.   He lingered in great
agony for a couple of days, giving from
time to time fragmentary and almost in-
coherent accounts of the dreadful catastrophe, and then passed on to join the rest
of his comrades beyond the grave.

As the massacre was complete, but little
can be told of the manner in which the
gallant soldiers fought against the overwhelming foe.   They died as soldiers
should, upholding to the last the honor
of their country and their profession.

A Daring Plunge.

"Daily toil, untended pain, danger ever by,
  Ah ! how many here have lain down like you to die ;
  Simply done your soldier's part through long months of woe,
  All endured with soldier's heart—battle, famine, snow."

IN the month of December, 1870, Lieutenant H. B. Mellen, of the Sixth
United States Cavalry, stationed at
Camp Wichita, received orders to repair
to Fort Richardson, Texas, for duty as a
member of a general court-martial. The
duty required a long ride across a dreary
country infested by roving bands of
Kiowas and Comanches. The weather,
even for the season of the year, was
extremely cold. Filling his haversack
with food, his pouch with cartridges, and
buckling on his revolvers, the lieutenant
mounted his horse, and, without escort
or guide, quite alone, pursued his solitary

179

ride all day. As evening drew on he came to a river, swollen with icy floods, which could only be crossed by swimming. He rode to the verge of the full stream. His intelligent steed calmly surveyed the situation. Extending his forelegs, he planted his front feet on the precipitous edge, lowered his head until his nose touched and tested the velocity and temperature of the rushing water, then straightened up, and, taking a long breath which made the saddle creak, he stood motionless, awaiting the verdict. Hesitation or delay would only have increased the risk, so the rider, patting his horse kindly on the neck, closed his knees tightly, raised the bridle hand, and, with a touch of the spur and a word of encouragement, plunged daringly into the chilling stream. Out of sight for a moment below the turbid waters, the horse arose bearing his rider, and, with a shake of the head, blowing the water from his nostrils and breathing aloud, the noble animal struck out bravely for the opposite shore. As he struggled to ascend the slippery bank, the treacherous mud under his feet gave way, and, toppling over, horse and rider fell back into the river.

The lieutenant was cumbered with his revolvers, ammunition, overcoat, and top-boots. He had the presence of mind to realize that his best chance for safety was to husband his strength and drift with the stream. His horse followed him closely. At length, chilled and exhausted, a sudden bend of the river enabled him through a great effort to grasp a friend-ly shrub on the bank, and by its aid he drew himself to shore, which was no sooner reached than he became insensible. He remained unconscious until far into the night. Then, recovering, he found his faithful horse standing—a patient sentinel—at his side. He endeavored to rise, but his feet were frozen in his boots, and his legs were benumbed and powerless. He sank to the ground, and, as the hours of torture and of agony dragged slowly on, again and again attempted to mount. But

his efforts were fruitless.   The day drew
to a close, but no one crossed his path
and not a glimpse of succor could be seen.
Night again enveloped the sufferer and
his patient horse—a sufferer too—and still
he was unable to reach the saddle.   The
pangs of hunger and of thirst were now
added to other tortures, and death itself
would have been a relief.

The second night and second day were
but a repetition of the first, and yet with
unsurpassed resolution and endurance the
brave lieutenant struggled again and again
to mount his steed.   For forty-eight hours,
without food, drink, or fire, did this heroic
struggle continue.

At last, as if the Fates had wearied of
their persecution, he succeeded, and soon
reached a camp occupied by hunters.
Word was promptly sent to Wichita, and
an ambulance, with a party including the
post surgeon, was at once despatched to
bring back their unfortunate comrade.
The thermometer at this time marked ten
degrees below zero, and several, including

the doctor, were badly frost-bitten before reaching the hunters' camp. The lieutenant, suffering intensely and on the verge of delirium, was conveyed quickly back to the post. Soon after his arrival he became insensible. The news which greeted him when consciousness returned was anything but cheering. His life could only be saved by amputating his right foot at the ankle-joint and by taking off the toes from the left foot. He quietly acquiesced, and the dangerous operation was performed. But it did not end there. The bones of the remaining heel became necrosed, a large ulcer formed which obstinately refused to yield to treatment, and it soon became necessary to amputate the left foot. Thus both feet were finally lost, and a valuable young officer, with promise of a bright career, was doomed to go on crutches for life, and passed from the active to the retired list of the army.

This narrative is not an exaggeration, but "an ower-true tale." The hero of it is still alive, though, like Ben Battle,

having lost his feet, he has been obliged
to lay down his arms.   Fiction can present no more pathetic incident.   The
summons to duty at a distant post; the
lonely ride; the swollen river; the gallant horse and rider breasting the turbid
waters; the sudden slip and the struggle
amid the icy waves; the grasp for life;
the long, dead blank; the painful awaken-
ing to a possible death from those terrible
foes, cold and starvation; the heroic efforts to gain the saddle; the agonizing
ride, and the final amputation of both
feet — all these are actual occurrences
growing out of the execution of a simple
order in the ordinary routine of the officer's life on the frontier.

When duty calls obedience is the watch-
word, even if it leads to certain death.
Those accustomed to cheerful homes and
uneventful lives can form at best but a
feeble conception of the hardships un-
dergone by the military pioneers of civilization.

Modoc Treachery.

"He was a man, take him for all in all,
I shall not look upon his like again."

ON Good Friday, the 11th of April, 1873, the direful news flashed through the land that the eminent patriot and soldier, Brigadier-General E. R. S. Canby, of the United States Army, had been treacherously murdered by "Modoc" Indians in the "Lava Beds" of Oregon. This victim was one of nature's noblemen. The various elements of his character—composed of the purest and finest materials—were perfectly adjusted. By rare cultivation he had risen above the ordinary weaknesses of human nature, but looked upon them in others, not with the intolerance of bigotry or self-righteousness, but with the smile of compassion and patience. In the profession of arms he was an infalli-

ble guide rather than a brilliant chief.
Whether in council or campaign, he was
the cloud by day and the pillar of fire by
night, which his hosts followed with abid-
ing faith, not blindly, as if dazzled by his
genius, but understandingly, fairly won
by his wisdom and justice.

A clear and pervading spirit of truth,
supported by superior acquirements in
matters of constitutional and statute law,
coupled with his high rank in the military
service, made him a peculiarly useful instrument in the restoration of public order
and the re-establishment of civil government after the war of the Rebellion had
closed. Wisdom, fidelity to principle, and
unfaltering devotion to duty marked his
administration in every sphere to which
he was called. Thirty-eight years of unre-
mitting professional toil, embracing the
Florida, Mexican, and Civil wars, in the
last of which he received a painful wound,
suggested a period of comparative repose
for this indefatigable public servant. In
response to this necessity he was, in the

year 1869, sent to the Pacific coast in command of the Department of the Columbia, with his headquarters at Portland, Oregon. It was expected that his duties would be mainly administrative and wholly peaceful; but periods of peace, as has been often demonstrated, are full of danger for officers of the army of the United States. And so it proved in his case. While on a mission to the Indians of the Northwest he fell a victim to their treachery and cruelty. With millions who read in the morning papers the sad intelligence of his death all was peaceful and quiet. But few had even heard of the "Modocs" or of the "Lava Beds," and fewer still knew that for weeks this gallant soldier's life had been at stake in the cause of justice between the white man and the savage.

The Modoc Indians are an offshoot of the Klamaths. They occupied a region near the line between Oregon and California known as the "Lost River Basin." The old government road to Oregon and

California passed through their country,
and difficulties sprang up between the
Modocs and the emigrants as soon as it
began to be travelled.   Many of the
former were killed and cruel butcheries
of the latter occurred.   The most re-
volting was the massacre of seventy-five
white persons in 1852.   The scene of this
horrible tragedy, on the margin of Tule
Lake, has ever since been known as
"Bloody Point."   Outrages by the Modocs reached such a pass that a company
of volunteers was organized in 1852 "for
the protection of emigrants," and took the
field against the offenders.   But failing
to bring them to battle, a "peace talk"
was proposed by the whites, and, after
some demur, accepted by the Indians.
Forty-six warriors responded and entrusted themselves to the good faith of the
white men.   The council was a prearranged slaughter-pen.   All save five of
the forty-six confiding Modocs were suddenly and brutally slain.   This act of
treachery dwelt in the memory of the

Modoc people. Its sting was sharpened
by the fact that the dastardly act was received with marked expressions of approval, and on his return to the settlements
the leader in the outrage was welcomed
with demonstrations, bonfires, and ban-
quets, and subsequently obtained the appointment of Indian Agent. The heathen
treasured up the example these Christians
set him. Outrages occurred from time to
time, and hostilities more or less extensive
continued until 1864, when a treaty was
made with the Klamaths, Yakooskin
Snakes, and Modocs, by which they were,
for a specified consideration, to give up
the country they claimed, and confine
themselves to a designated area in Oregon,
known as the Klamath Reservation. In
compliance with the agreement the Modocs took up their abode on the reservation, and went to work with zeal to build
cabins and enclose ground for cultivation.
But in consequence, mainly, of annoyance
from their enemies, the Klamaths, who
largely outnumbered them, they left in a

few months and returned to their old homes. The treaty, though approved by the Senate in 1866, was not finally ratified until the 10th of December, 1869, and then with amendments. In the meantime the Indians had grown suspicious, and when the amended treaty was made known to them some of the Modocs denied that it conformed to the agreement, but yielded at the time a reluctant assent to its provisions. That part of the Modoc band which had followed Captain Jack was still absent from the reservation, but, on promises of assistance and assurances that they would be protected from the Klamaths, they returned to it in 1869, and again earnestly entered upon arrangements for making homes and carrying out their part of the contract. But the Klamaths resumed their insults and annoyances, taunted the Modocs with being strangers, orphans, poor men, etc., and claimed tribute for the timber, fish, grass, and water. The Modocs appealed to the Indian Agent in charge for the protection which had been pledged, but, instead of affording it, the Agent removed the band to another locality, leaving them to pocket the insults and bear as they best could the loss of the work already done. The Klamaths were emboldened by this action, and the Modocs were no sooner established and fairly at work on new ground than exactions from their powerful oppressors, taunts, and interferences were renewed in aggravated form, and an appeal for justice was again submitted. Instead of a rebuke to the offenders, another move of the injured party was ordered. The leader sought carefully for a suitable resting-place for his followers. Not finding it on the reservation, they fled to their old homes. But their title had been surrendered, and during their absence the white settlers in that region had increased; there was not room for both races, and complaints arose.

In 1871 the Superintendent of Indian Affairs sent Commissioners to confer with the Modocs and try and induce them to

return to the reservation; but they steadfastly refused, and secured authority from
the Commissioners to remain where they
were until the Superintendent could see
them. This was understood by the Indians as a settlement of the question until some permanent arrangement could be
made. They claimed that they should be
established on a small reservation on Lost
River, separate and distinct from the Klamaths. Knowing they had lost their title
in common to their lands, the principal
men among them took into serious consideration the question of dissolving their
tribal relations and taking up lands in
severalty as other claimants did. They
were in constant communication with
the whites, and consulted attorneys in
reference to establishing land claims.
But they were likely to be troublesome
neighbors, and the whites urged their
removal, and brought forward arguments and pretexts to secure that end.
Indeed, in the latter part of the month
of June, 1871, the Indian Agent requested

the commander of Fort Klamath to have
Captain Jack, the chief, arrested for murder.   He had killed an Indian doctor—a
medicine man—by shooting him through
the head when asleep, for failing to cure
his little child of some illness.   It was not
deemed best to bring on hostilities with
the tribe by immediately arresting him, so
measures were taken to capture him at
Yreka, California, whither he generally
repaired on the Fourth of July and other
gala days to have a good time.   A detachment of cavalry was sent to Yreka for
the purpose ; but the wily Jack, knowing
his liability to arrest and having got scent
of his danger, kept away on this occasion,
and so the attempt to secure him proved
abortive.

No serious offences of recent date appear to have been committed by the other
members of the tribe, but there were mis-
demeanors and threats to complain of,
and these were presented with much feeling and formality.   In January, 1872, an
affidavit was sent to the military autho-

rities, setting forth that Modoc Indians came to a settler's house, knocked down fences around a haystack and turned their ponies in, and also took hay to their wigwams, and that they stole household utensils and threatened the lives of white men. A large number of the settlers in the Modoc country joined in a petition to have these Indians forced to the reservation by the United States troops. The Superintendent of Indian Affairs for Oregon united with the settlers, and in this shape the subject went before General Canby, the department commander. After alluding to the facts in the case that eminent soldier responded :

"In the summer of last year, and in consequence of complaints against these Indians, the Superintendent sent commissioners to confer with them, who authorized the Modocs to remain where they were until the Superintendent could see them. This has been understood as a settlement of the question until some permanent arrangement could be made for them, and, unless they have violated some subsequent agreement, I do not think that the immediate application of force, as asked for, would be either expedient or just. They should, at least, be notified that a new location has been selected for them and provision made for their wants. They should also be allowed reasonable and definite time to remove their families, and fully warned that their refusal or failure to remove to the reservation within the appointed time would be followed by such measures as may be necessary to compel them. I am not surprised at the unwillingness of the Modocs to return to any point of the reservation where they would be exposed to the hostilities and annoyances they have heretofore experienced (and without adequate protection) from the Klamaths; but they have expressed a desire to be established on Lost River, where they would be free from this trouble, and the Superintendent informed me last summer that he would endeavor to secure such a location for them. In no

other respect are the Modocs entitled to
much consideration, and although many
of the complaints against them have been
found to be greatly exaggerated, they are,
without being absolutely hostile, sufficiently troublesome to keep up a constant feeling of apprehension among the settlers."

Unfortunately the wise and just views expressed by General Canby were not accept-
able to the complainants nor to the Indian
Agent, and he who thus earnestly urged
justice to the savage became the most conspicuous victim of his blind ferocity.

The Agent, responding to the wishes of
the whites, urged upon the Commissioner
of Indian Affairs in Washington that these
Indians be forced back to the hateful
Klamath Reservation, and the Commissioner responded : " You are directed to remove the Modoc Indians to Camp Yainax,
on Klamath Reservation, peaceably if you
possibly can, but forcibly if you must."
And, notwithstanding General Canby's
views, the Agent, in the latter part of November, 1872, made a peremptory demand

on the Modocs to return to the detested spot. They defiantly refused, whereupon the Agent wrote to the commander of Fort Klamath, the nearest military post, setting forth the facts and saying : "To carry out instructions from the Commissioner of Indian Affairs, I have to request that you at once furnish a sufficient force to compel said Indians to go to Camp Yainax on said reservation. I transfer the whole matter to your department, without presuming to dictate the course you shall pursue in executing the order aforesaid, hoping that you may accomplish the object desired without shedding blood, if possible to avoid it. If it shall become necessary to use force, then I have to request that you arrest Captain Jack, Black Jim, and Scarfaced Charley, and hold them subject to my orders."

This was the immediate cause of the Modoc War. The officer to whom the appeal for force was made ordered as follows on the 28th of November, 1872 :

"In compliance with the request of the

Superintendent of Indian Affairs for Oregon, dated Link River, November 27, 1872, Captain James Jackson, First Cavalry, with all the available men of his troop, will proceed at once, *via* Link River, to Captain Jack's camp of Modoc Indians, endeavoring to get there before to-morrow morning ; and if any opposition is offered on the part of the Modoc Indians to the requirements of the Superintendent, he will arrest, if possible, Captain Jack, Black Jim, and Scar-faced Charley. He will endeavor to accomplish all of this without bloodshed, if possible ; but if the Indians persist in refusing to obey the orders of the Government, he will use such force as may be necessary to compel them to do so ; and the responsibility must rest on the Indians who defy the authority of the Government."

The demand for troops was made by the Agent, and filled by the commander at Fort Klamath, without General Canby's knowledge. Captain Jack's band was at this time estimated to contain from sixty to eighty warriors, but the smaller figure exceeded the actual number. Captain Jack, Schonchin John, Scar-faced Charley, and eleven or twelve others, with their families, were encamped on the west, while Curly-headed Doctor, Hooker Jim, and nine other warriors, with their families, occupied the east bank of Lost River, a deep stream three hundred feet wide. These Indians passed freely to and fro through the settlements, hunted in the mountains, and traded in the neighboring towns. They were well known to the community. Some of them spoke the English language, and the most noted went by the names, or nicknames, given to them by the whites. They were "troublesome," as the lower orders in other sections are, but not at war, and had no knowledge or intimation of the hostile enterprise which was about to destroy them.

Captain Jackson's troop of the First United States Cavalry made the march required of it on the cold and rainy night of the 28th of November, 1872, and, using

that officer's words, "*jumped* the camp of
Captain Jack's Modoc Indians soon after
daylight" on the morning of the 29th.
Forming line, "they moved down on the
camp at a trot, completely surprising the
Indians, and causing great commotion
among them." The Captain demanded
that they surrender and disarm. A brief
parley was held. A conflict ensued. It
is said the Indians fired the first shot; but
that is doubtful, and the matter is not important, considering the attitude assumed
by the whites. The struggle had begun.
Captain Jackson said of it: "I immediately poured volley after volley among the
hostile Indians, took their camp, killed
eight or nine warriors, and drove the rest
into the hills (only the squaws remained,
bewailing their dead and wounded braves).
During the engagement I lost one man
killed and seven wounded, three of the
last severely, and perhaps dangerously.
My force was too weak to pursue and
capture the Indians that made off, owing
to the necessity of taking care of my

wounded and protecting the few citizens who had collected at Crawley's Ranch. The Indians were all around us, and, apprehensive of a rear attack, I destroyed Captain Jack's camp and crossed to the other side of the river by the ford, a march of fifteen miles, taking post at Crawley's Ranch, where I now am. I need reinforcements and orders as to future course."

As Captain Jackson, during the night of the 28th, advanced upon the encampment on the west, a party of citizens, by what authority or instigation is not known, surrounded and attacked the encampment on the east bank of Lost River, and made a demand for its surrender. This resulted in an engagement between the Indians of that encampment and the citizens. The latter were repulsed and sought " the refuge of Crawley's Ranch," as the troops had done. Thus ended the first move towards forcing the Modocs back to the Klamath Reservation. The result was not encouraging. The conflict which the sagacious Canby had labored so earnestly to prevent was fully inaugurated, not only between the Indians and the troops, but also between them and the citizens among whom they had been living. The Indians fled to the "Lava Beds," the safest refuge in the land. "The location is the most inaccessible the country affords, and one man fairly secreted in it is more than equal to twenty engaged in trying to ferret him out." It is to the south of Tule Lake (one of three lakes, Lower Klamath, Tule, and Clear Lake, which are eight miles apart). Crevices and gorges of the Lava Beds, communicating with the lake, afforded the Modocs an abundant supply of water. The Lost River, on the banks of which stood their old homes, empties into the head of Tule Lake, and they knew every foot of the country. Their refuge was far too extensive for investment by the force available, and they could steal out for food and plunder and return through the secret passages.

Language fails to convey a correct con-

ception of this remarkable formation. It
is about four miles wide by seven long,
and presents the appearance on first view
of an immense sage-bush plain, with no
obstructions to easy movement in every
direction. A closer examination, however, develops the fact that this plain is
broken at irregular intervals by sections
of low, rocky ridges. The ridges are not
isolated, but occur in groups, and form
perfect networks of obstructions, admi-
rably adapted to defence by an active
enemy; they seldom rise to a height of
more than twenty feet above the general
level of the bed, and are, as a rule, split
open at the top, giving continuous cover
along the crests. Transversal crevices furnished excellent communications, through
which the Indians passed from one ridge
to the other without the least exposure.
Only a few of these cross-passages and
insecure positions, sufficient to satisfy the
requirements of free communication, were
left open by the savages in that series of
ridges which made up "Jack's Strong-

hold." The rest were in all cases block-
aded by rolling in heavy rocks. The formation, as described, does not cover the
entire area of the Lava Beds. It occurs
in patches of greater or less extent. Sepa-
rating these patches are comparatively
even sage-bush plains, which do not afford
good defensive positions. These plains,
however, are difficult to move over, by
reason of the number of rocks covering
them, as well as the continual recurrence
of deep, rocky depressions or ravines,
which cannot be detected generally until
their borders are reached. As can readily
be imagined, the movement of troops
across these portions, when in the vicinity
of the ridges, requires the utmost caution,
for with no good cover they are liable to
be surprised by the fire of a perfectly
concealed enemy, and if cover be sought
in the depressions, in the end the place of
refuge will prove to be a slaughter-pen for
those in it.

The greater portion of the defensive line
was one of those cracks or crevices re-

ferred to, and where this natural rifle-pit
terminated the line was continued by
building stone walls four or five feet in
height. In this way, by a combination of
natural and artificial works, the Indian position was fortified on all sides. "Jack's
Cave," a place of which the most exaggerated accounts were written, is the least
important feature of the position: a ver-
tical pit of about twelve or fifteen feet in
diameter, spreading out at its base in one
direction, so as to leave that portion
arched. Being in it, security from distant
fire was obtained, but no defence could be
made from it.

But to resume. Success was with the
Indians. The aspect of affairs was serious.
Reinforcements, *ammunition,* and other
supplies were ordered up, and the commanding officer of the District of the
Lakes, embracing the several posts within
the theatre of war, took the field in person. The Indians, in this instance as in
so many others, were underrated. On the
26th of December the district commander

reported: "If the ammunition on hand had been sufficient and warranted me in doing so, I would have ordered the attack on about the 27th of December; but the howitzers and ammunition for small arms will reach us at about the same time, and we will be prepared to *make short work of this impudent and enterprising savage.* I feel confident the guns will astonish and terrify them, and perhaps save much close skirmishing and loss of life. I do not think the citizens are in danger, and, *unless the Modocs crawl off south through the Lava Beds on our approach, we hope to make short work of them very soon* after our ammunition comes up."

He reported on the 15th of January, 1873: "I am happy to announce that after all our annoying delays *we are now in better condition than I ever saw troops for a movement against hostile Indians.* Within thirty-six hours after Lieutenant Miller, First Cavalry, reached me with the howitzers, a well-selected and very efficient gun detachment were handling them to the infinite delight of the volunteers. They would not have remained a day longer than January 6 had not they been certain that the guns were coming. We leave for Captain Jack's 'Gibraltar' to-morrow morning, and a more enthusiastic, jolly set of regulars and volunteers I never had the pleasure to command. *If the Modocs will only try to make good their boast to whip a thousand soldiers, all will be satisfied.* Our scouts and friendly Indians insist that the Modocs will fight us desperately, but *I don't understand how they can think of attempting any serious resistance*, though, of course, we are prepared for their fight or flight."

How much the commander had underestimated the enemy may be inferred from his report of January 19, in which he says :

"We attacked the Modocs on the 17th with about four hundred good men, two hundred and twenty-five of them regulars. We fought the Indians through the 'Lava

Beds' to their stronghold, which is in the centre of miles of rocky fissures, caves, crevices, gorges, and ravines, some of them one hundred feet deep. In the opinion of any experienced officer of regulars or volunteers, one thousand men would be required to dislodge them from their almost impregnable position with a free use of mortar batteries. No troops could have fought better than all did, advancing cheerfully against an unseen enemy over the roughest rock-country imaginable. *The troops have withdrawn to their camps.* The volunteers will probably go out of service very soon. We will use our force to cut off raiding Modocs, and operate against them in every way possible until *reinforcements arrive.* Our loss in killed and wounded is about forty. *I have never before encountered an enemy, civilized or savage, occupying a position of such great natural strength as the Modoc stronghold, nor have I ever seen troops engage a better armed or more skilful foe.*"

Thus failed the second effort to force the Modocs back to the Klamath Reservation.

While additional forces were taking the field, the authorities in Washington considered the state of affairs, and at the most unsuitable period of the struggle resolved to turn the management over to Peace Commissioners. On the 29th of January the Secretary of the Interior addressed a letter to his subordinate, the Commissioner of Indian Affairs, in which he said: "Referring to the difficulties that have arisen, and still continue to exist between the troops of the United States and the Modoc Indians in Oregon, I have to inform you that I have determined to send a Commission to the scene of the difficulty for the purpose of examining into the same. This Commission will consist of three members whose names will hereafter be furnished to you. It will be required to proceed to the Modoc country as rapidly as possible, and, before entering upon the active discharge of its

duties, will confer with General Canby, of
the United States Army, and in all subsequent proceedings of the Commission it
should confer freely with that officer, and
act under his advice as far as it may be
possible to do so, and always with his cooperation. The objects to be obtained by
this Commission are these: First, to ascertain the causes which have led to the
difficulties and hostilities between the
troops and the Modocs; and, secondly, to
devise the most effective and judicious
measures for preventing the continuance
of these hostilities, and for the restoration
of peace." The letter also set forth the
advisability of removing the Modoc Indians, "with their consent," to some *new*
reservation, and the "desire of the Department in this as well as in all other
cases of like character to conduct its communications with the Indians in such
manner as to secure peace and obtain
their confidence, if possible, and their
voluntary consent to a compliance with
such regulations as may be deemed ne-

cessary for their present and future welfare.''

It is fair to infer from this artful letter that the Department of the Interior deprecated hostilities, that it sought to mediate between the troops and the Indians, and that it was not responsible for the existing conflict, and was even ignorant of the cause of it. Justice to the Army, and especially to General Canby, calls for the truth on these points.

These hostilities were due to the failure of the Indian Department to provide properly for the Modocs under the treaty, and to protect them from the Klamaths when they were on the reservation. They were precipitated by the instructions of the Commissioner of Indian Affairs ''to remove the Modoc Indians to Camp Yainax, on Klamath Reservation, peaceably if you possibly can, but forcibly if you must.'' This terse and positive order was made after General Canby had reported that the Modocs ought not to be forced back to the *Klamath* Reservation, but that they should be notified of a *new* reservation, and be allowed a reasonable "and definite time to remove their families," and that the immediate application of force would be neither expedient nor just. The war order of the Commissioner did not contemplate for the Modocs the "new" reservation, the removal with "their consent," the conducting of communications with them "*in such manner as to secure peace and gain their confidence*" which the foregoing letter, written by the Secretary of the Interior long after the Indian Bureau had created the war, sets forth so prominently.

General Canby was above crimination or recrimination. Instead of complaining of the departure from his views which brought on hostilities, he excused it as well as he could, and undertook to treat wisely and effectually the evils which others had brought about. In his judgment vigor was now as necessary to end the difficulties as moderation had been to prevent them. On the 30th of January he telegraphed the General of the Army: "I have been very solicitous that these Indians should be fairly treated, and have repeatedly used military force lest they might be wronged, until their claims or pretensions were decided by proper authority. That having been done, I think they should now be treated as any other criminals, and *that there will be no peace in that part of the frontier until they are subdued and punished.*"

But he was thwarted in prosecuting, as he had been in preventing, the war. On the 30th and 31st of January the General of the Army telegraphed Canby: "The President seems disposed to allow the peace men to try their hands on Captain Jack. Let all defensive measures proceed. It is the desire of the President that you use the troops to protect the inhabitants as against the Modoc Indians, but, if possible, to avoid war"; and on the 3d of February the instructions to "keep the troops on the defensive" were repeated.

That he might confer with the Peace

Commissioners, as required by instructions, and at the same time give personal
attention to the delicate operation of so
using the troops as to preserve the defensive, protect the inhabitants, and avoid
war, General Canby joined his forces in
person at the "Lava Beds," on the 16th
of February. The Commission—Mr. A. B.
Meacham at the head of it—arrived soon
after, and opened communication with the
enemy. By the 24th of March it seems
that the confidence reposed in the Commission by the Department of the Interior
had been transferred entirely to General
Canby. On that date the General of the
Army telegraphed him as follows: "Secretary Delano is in possession of all your
despatches up to March 16; and he ad-
vises the Secretary of War that he is so
impressed with your wisdom and desire to
fulfil the peaceful policy of the Government that he authorizes you to remove
from the present Commission any members you think unfit, to appoint others to
their places, and to report through us to

him such changes. This actually devolves on you the entire management of the Modoc question, and the Secretary of War instructs me to give you his sanction and approval."

The Commission, however, during the entire period of its presence on the field, had been conducting negotiations, and General Canby did not find it best to exercise additional power over it under the foregoing authorization. The appointment of a Commission by the highest power in the land to sue for peace at this stage of affairs had of itself an unfavorable effect upon the Indians in their attitude towards the Government. This was probably somewhat increased by the anxiety for peace which the Commission, under the spur of the Interior Department, exhibited to the savages at the beginning of negotiations. The first message to the Indians was: "We come in good faith to make peace. Our hearts are all for peace; no act of war will be allowed while peace-talks are being had; no move-

ments of troops will be made." The Indians began to think, and with good
reason, we were afraid of them. They
answered to the message that they wanted peace, but were unwilling to come out
of the Lava Beds. Judge Steele, of Yreka, California, in whom they reposed
great confidence, made two visits to their
strongholds to try and induce them to
come out for a council. They evaded,
prevaricated, resisted ; and he escaped
with his life only through the friendship
of Captain Jack, Scar-faced Charley, and
two others, who stood guard over him
throughout the last night he spent in
their camp. On his return he warned
the Commission of the danger, and expressed the opinion that no meeting could
be had, no peace could be made. "My
advice," he says, "to General Canby and
the Peace Commissioners, on my return
from the cave the last time, was that all
negotiations should cease until the Indians should become the soliciting party.
I told them, further, that my opinion was

that they thought our people afraid of them, and that they were carrying on the negotiations with a hope to get Gen. Canby and Col. Gillem, Messrs. Meacham and Applegate, in their power, and in such an event they would certainly kill them all."

While the Commission was deliberating upon its further proceedings a delegation from the Modocs, headed by Mary, Captain Jack's sister, appeared, and announced that if wagons were sent to bring them in the whole band would surrender on terms which had been mentioned to them. The proposition was accepted and a day named, but before the time came another delegation arrived, made apologies for failure, and sought delay. Another day was fixed, with the assurance from General Canby that, in case of further failure, measures would be taken to compel compliance. Again the Indians failed, but this time made no apology.

In the meantime it did not escape the Indian vigilance that General Canby (acting under his instructions to protect the in-

habitants) was drawing his military cordon
more tightly around them, and that one
of the subordinate commanders had captured and taken away a herd of their ponies ; this notwithstanding the fact that
in the first communication from the Commissioners they were assured that no act
of war would be allowed while peace-talks
were being had, and that no movements of
troops would be made.

General Canby reported on the 17th of
March : "Troops are being removed into
positions which will make it difficult for
them [the Indians] to secure egress for
raiding purposes. I hope by this not only
to secure the settlers but to impress the
Indians with the folly of resistance." On
the 24th of March he reported in the same
connection : "The troops are now moving
into their positions" ; and on the 28th of
the same month he added : "I think when
the avenues of escape are closed, and their
supplies cut off or abridged, they will
come in."

These movements, as well as the evidences and apprehensions of treachery, were reported to the Secretary of the Interior in Washington. On the 5th of March he telegraphed the Commission: "I do not believe the Modocs mean treachery. The mission should not be a failure. I think I understand their unwillingness to confide in you. Continue negotiations."

Efforts were continued, and on the 2d of April a meeting with the Indians was effected, but nothing was agreed upon except that a council-tent should be erected about three-quarters of a mile from the headquarters of the troops on the trail leading to the fastnesses of the Indians.

Among the attachés of the Commission was Frank Riddle, an interpreter, a man of much intelligence and courage. He had lived for many years in the Modoc country, and was well versed in the language and habits of the tribe. While residing amongst them he had married a full-blooded Modoc, of more than ordinary personal attractions and intelligence.

She loved her white husband, and, In·
dian to the core, knew no law but his
will and wish. She wandered with him
through scenes of danger and of hardship,
and his welfare and comfort were ever
foremost in her thoughts. Holding the
confidence of the whites, and, strange to
say, trusted also by the Modocs, Tobe, as
she was called, passed as an envoy from
one camp to the other, and had full opportunity of observing the disposition of
the occupants of the Lava Beds. The taci-
turn savages, however, were careful not
to give by word or sign in her presence the
least intimation of their intentions. But
with the shrewdness of her sex and wild
race, sharpened by her perilous position,
she scented danger in the quiet air, and
took in through her quickened senses the
unwhispered plots of her tribe. Though
she could reveal no proofs to sustain the
belief, she insisted that there was treachery in the air around the Lava Beds. A
confidant as it appeared in her evidence
on the trial, hereinafter mentioned, had

dropped a word of warning in her ear, and she was watchful; she could not be deceived; but, unfortunately, she was unable to convince her more intelligent listeners. Her fidelity and rare acuteness had served her husband in many a dangerous adventure, and he had learned to believe her without requiring reasons. He adopted her conclusions, and joined in her entreaties to the Commissioners and commander not to place confidence in the pledges and promises of the Modocs, but to be prepared at all points to resist premeditated treachery. "I know she is right," said Riddle; "I have been married to her for twelve years, and she has never in all that time deceived or told me a lie."

But the warnings went unheeded. Negotiations and the peace policy must be pursued, and were pursued to the bitter end. The Secretary of the Interior had announced from his high place in Washington that the negotiations must proceed, he did "not believe the Modocs

meant treachery." His subordinates at
the foot of the Lava Beds and in the very
sight of the Indians accepted the dictum
and stumbled on half-blindly to their fate.
It was not in Tobe's power to overcome the
weight of authority.

The Commission as organized at this
time consisted of A. B. Meacham, Rev.
Dr. Thomas, and L. S. Dyar, Indian Agent.
The negotiations for a council meeting
having failed so far, General Canby again
tightened the cordon of troops and moved
his headquarters to the foot of the bluffs,
about two miles from the Modoc stronghold.

On the 4th of April, at the request of
Captain Jack, Mr. Meacham had a meeting with him at the council-tent. The
Modoc chief was accompanied by six
warriors and the women of his own family ; Mr. Meacham by Judge Roseborough
and J. A. Fairchilds, and Riddle and his
wife, Tobe, as interpreters. The savage's
bearing was haughty and offensive, his
language positive and declamatory. He

would not listen patiently, declaring he could never live in peace with the Klamaths, but wanted a home, "just the same as a white man, on Lost River." On being told that he could not have a home there he said : "I give up home ; give me this lava bed. No white man will ever want it." He then went on to say that "the law was all on one side, was made by the white man for white men, leaving the Indian all out," and finally announced he could not control his people, and would die with them if peace was not made. The meeting broke up unsatisfactorily. It strengthened Tobe's conviction that danger was impending. On the 5th of April she was sent into the Modoc camp with a proposition to Captain Jack to surrender on favorable terms, with such others as might wish to do so. He declined the offer. She returned, more settled than ever in the belief that mischief was hatching, and again she warned the Commissioners and General Canby ; but, alas ! she had not the power of language to

convince them. Every effort at negotiation now seemed exhausted on our part,
and General Canby was on the eve of re-
sorting to sterner measures when, on the
8th of April, a messenger visited the Commission, asking for a "peace-talk," saying
that six unarmed Modocs were at the
council-tent in the Lava Beds, anxious to
make peace and requesting the Commission to meet them. The signal officer at
the station overlooking the Lava Beds reported the "six Indians, and also in the
rocks behind them *twenty other Indians,
all armed.*" Treachery was evident, and
no meeting was had. Further councils appeared useless and unsafe. But on the
morning of the 10th of April a delegation
from the Modoc camp, consisting of Boston Charley and Bogus Charley, arrived,
with a request for a meeting. The proposition was that the Commission, including General Canby and Colonel Gillem
(the latter in immediate command of the
troops), should come next day to the
council-tent, *unarmed*, to meet a *like num-*

ber of *unarmed* Modocs. The Modocs
would then all come to headquarters and
surrender on the day following. The
wily envoys, Boston and Bogus, were well
chosen. Under the cover of good intentions and fair promises they concealed
their villanous designs. The long examination and cross-examination to which
they were subjected failed to develop a
trace of the treachery they were practising. But though nothing could be detected, an undefined dread had arisen
among some of the Commissioners. Notwithstanding she was too rude of speech
to convince, the earnestness of Tobe's
manner had produced an impression ; but
its effect was defeated by the cunning and
assumed sincerity of the Indian envoys,
and by the desire known to exist in the
Interior Department for a settlement by
negotiation. Boston and Bogus Charley
accepted the white man's hospitality,
and remained that night in camp,
breakfasting the next morning with
Dr. Thomas. Dr. Thomas had done

many favors to Boston Charley, and he had been treated like a brother in the church. How the kindness extended to him was rewarded the sequel will show.

The fatal morning of Friday, April 11, had arrived. A consultation was again held as to keeping the appointment. Dr. Thomas said it was a *duty* that *must* be performed. General Canby remarked that the importance of the object in view justified taking some risk, and added that a strict watch had been kept from the signal station and only *five* Indians, unarmed, were at the council-tent ; that the watch would be continued, and in the event of an attack the troops would come to the rescue. Commissioners Meacham and Dyar, more fully impressed with the peril involved, protested against the meeting, and finally proposed that a force sufficient for protection should be taken. But both General Canby and Dr. Thomas objected, saying it would be a breach of faith, and both of these courageous and conscientious men refused to agree that during the meeting *any promise which could not be kept* should be made the Indians, even if necessary to avert danger. Riddle and his faithful wife now appeared and made an earnest appeal against the meeting, and, finding they could not prevent it, claimed that they should be relieved of all responsibility for the consequences. Yet, with full consciousness of the danger, this man and wife went bravely forward to share the fate from which they could not rescue their companions. All started for the ill-starred rendezvous: General Canby (carrying a box of cigars) and Dr. Thomas in advance on foot, accompanied by Boston Charley, followed by Meacham, Dyar, and Tobe on horseback, and Riddle on foot (Colonel Gillem was sick and unable to go).

On arriving at the council-tent six *armed* Indian leaders were met: Captain Jack, Schonchin, Shacknasty Jim, Ellen's Man, Hooker Jim, and Black Jim. Their pistols, though but poorly concealed under their loose and scanty garments, could not be seen by the observer at the signal station.   Boston and Bogus Charley, who had stayed all night with the troops, silently joined their comrades, and now the Commissioners, unarmed and helpless, found themselves confronted by eight armed savages.   Treachery was too evident to be doubted.   The white men were entrapped and at the mercy of those who know no mercy.   To have evinced a knowledge of the intended treachery would but have precipitated the assassination. Every man seemed to realize instinctively that an unsuspicious and undaunted mien afforded the only hope of escape.   Calmly and courageously the Commissioners and the General advanced towards the Indians.   On meeting, all sat down about a little fire of sage-brush, the white men on one side and the savages on the other.

General Canby was on the right, nearest the tent, seated on a stone ; on his left, Mr. Meacham ; still to his left, and a little in the rear, Dr. Thomas ; and close to Dr. Thomas, and slightly in front, Tobe, lying

down between Meacham and Thomas.
Opposite to and facing General Canby was
Schonchin; on his right, Captain Jack;
and, still to his right, Bogus Charley and
Boston Charley; Commissioner Dyar had
taken a position in front and a little to
the right of General Canby, and to the
left and rear of Schonchin; he sat on the
ground holding his horse; Ellen's Man,
Hooker Jim, and Shacknasty Jim were
seated at another small fire to the right
and rear. Boston Charley and Black Jim
walked about during the entire interview.
The interpreter, Riddle, stood near his
wife.

Soon after the council opened an incident occurred which was pregnant with
meaning. Hooker Jim walked up to
Dyar's horse, took an overcoat from the
saddle, and put it on, saying: "I am
Meacham now." The Commissioners
knew it was an insult and designed to
produce a disturbance. Mr. Meacham,
however, instead of resenting, said very
quietly: "Take my hat, too." The

Indian replied in his native tongue: "I will very soon." The storm was coming. These were but its mutterings. The actors in the lamentable affair were all in their places. The tragedy went on quickly to its murderous ending.

General Canby, now fully aware of the peril, arose, and with marked politeness handed cigars to the Indians and whites, and all, save Dr. Thomas, began to smoke. The General then said: "The President sent the soldiers here to see that everything is done right; they are your friends and will not harm you. I have had much experience with Indians. When a young man I was sent to remove a tribe from Florida to a new home west of the Mississippi River, and although they did not like me well at first, they did after they became acquainted, and they elected me a chief and gave me a name which meant 'the Indian's friend.' I was sent to remove another tribe to a new home, and they called me the 'Tall Man.' I visited both these tribes years afterwards, and they received me in a friendly way. I have no doubt that some time you Modoc people will receive me as kindly."

The Indians treated these remarks with contempt, and laughed as they were delivered.

Dr. Thomas then, on his knees, said : "I believe the Great Spirit put it in the heart of the President to send us here to make peace. I have known General Canby fourteen years, Mr. Meacham eighteen years, Mr. Dyar four years. I know all their hearts are good, and I know my own heart. We want no more war. The Great Spirit made all men. He made the red man and white man. He sees all our hearts and knows all we do. We are all brothers, and must live in peace together."

Captain Jack said but little. He was determined that he would not go to the reservation to be starved, saying : "Kill with bullet don't hurt much ; starve to death hurt a heap."

The impatient and blood-thirsty Schonchin arose, and in a violent tone, and with frequent repetitions, growing louder and louder, insisted that the soldiers should be taken away and that Hot Creek be given the Modocs for a home. While he was speaking, with no apparent purpose but to kill time and raise an excitement, two Modoc warriors, Barncho and Sloluck, suddenly appeared from behind a ridge of rocks some fifty yards away, each with three rifles in his arms. A signal had been given to these two Indians, as well as to those at the council, letting them know that a prearranged attack had been made on the troops posted on the farther side of the Lava Beds, and that the time for the massacre had arrived. Captain Jack arose quickly, slipped behind Dyar's horse for concealment while he drew and cocked his pistol. Sloluck and Barncho rushed on, followed by Steamboat Frank and Scar-faced Charley, both armed. All arose hastily, and General Canby demanded: "Captain Jack, what does this mean?" The Indian's answer was, "*A-ta Kantuxe*"—All ready—as he

sprang to within a few feet of the General
and snapped a revolver in his face. In an
instant the pistol was recocked, fired,
and the fatal bullet entered beneath the
left eye. The assault was the work of
a moment. The victims were helpless.
General Canby rushed forward for about
forty yards, then received another bullet
in his head from the rifle of Ellen's Man,
and fell backward dead. His clothing and
valuables were quickly taken by his assas-
sin, and his naked body left upon the
ground. At the command "*A-ta Kantuxe*" Boston Charley attacked Doctor
Thomas, whose bread he had eaten and
whose blessing he had received that morning. After falling from a gun-shot in the
breast, the doctor arose to his knees, supported himself with his right hand, and,
seeing the murderer over him, said in pite-
ous tones: "Don't shoot again, Boston; I
shall die anyway," but the fiend replied:
"God damn ye! may be so you believe
what squaw [Tobe] tell ye next time," and
shot him through the brain.

These are the sickening atrocities of so-called times of peace.

Commissioner Dyar fled, pursued by Hooker Jim, but luckily went unscathed. Riddle also escaped unhurt. Schonchin attacked Mr. Meacham, and, assisted by Shacknasty Jim and Black Jim, pursued and shot him several times while running. At about fifty yards from the tent he fell, and the Indians left him for dead. Boston Charley, however, eager for a trophy, returned and made preparations to scalp him ; but Tobe, who had by this time recovered from a blow given merely to stun her, with ready wit frustrated his fell purpose by running up and shouting with all her might, "The soldiers are coming," when the dastardly scalper fled in alarm. All of these events, so full of dire import, occupied but a few minutes. The attack had been seen from the signal station on the bluff west of the camp. The troops advanced at double-quick, but the desperate work was over. The savages, having glutted their vengeance, had fled to their "stronghold" in the Lava Beds. The "peace men," as General Sherman called them, had "tried their hands on Captain Jack." Negotiation was brought to a violent and bloody end. All thought of making terms with the Indians was now abandoned. Their destruction was a foregone conclusion. General Jeff. C. Davis, an energetic officer of the regular army, then at Indianapolis, was ordered at once to the command of the Department of Columbia, and hastened to the Lava Beds. Orders authorizing the swift and summary punishment of the outlaws were promptly issued by the War Department. The country was aroused, and no proceedings seemed too severe or too speedy.

But the criminals yet lay defiant in their stronghold. On the 15th of April a determined attack was begun on their lines by Colonel Gillem's forces, the fight lasting three days. The troops on the east and west of the Lava Beds formed a junction on the lake front, thus cutting off the supply of water, so much

depended upon by the Indians. They
were by this means compelled to abandon
their position ; but the troops were worn
out and dispirited, and the pursuit was
not vigorous. The savages found safer
refuge in another gorge, and again stood
at bay. The desperate siege was renewed,
and again with disastrous result. On the
26th of April Captain Evan Thomas, of
the Fourth United States Artillery, was
ordered to make a reconnoissance of the
enemy's position. His command consisted of five commissioned officers besides a
doctor, sixty-five enlisted men, and fourteen Warm Spring Indians. The command left camp at seven A.M. ; at noon it
reached the designated point and halted
for rest and refreshment. No Indians had
been met, no resistance was expected, and,
strange to say, a feeling of security prevailed among the officers of the expedition. Suddenly a few shots in close proximity announced the presence of the
enemy. It was a surprise. The officers
immediately sprang up and prepared for

action. The suddenness of the attack, however, and the well-directed fire of the Indians had somewhat demoralized the enlisted men, and many of them scattered and ran. The officers rallied the few brave spirits, mostly non-commissioned officers, who remained, and, gallantly facing the foe, they fought and died upon the spot.

All the commissioned officers of the artillery (Captain Thomas and Lieutenants Howe, Wright, Cranston, and Harris) were killed, the four former dying on the field and the latter while being carried from it. The doctor, Bernard G. Semig, received a wound in the shoulder early in the fight which paralyzed the right arm. He was soon afterwards wounded in the left leg (resulting in amputation) and left on the field. He lay there for forty hours, when he was found by a scouting party of our troops sent out to ascertain the fate of the command. The Indians, though near at hand, could not reach him over the gorges and chasms without exposing themselves to the view of the troops. The extraordinary features of the Lava Beds, which had enabled the surprise and destruction of the troops, now, in turn, served to protect this mutilated remnant of the ill-fated party.

The Indian had again triumphed and wreaked a bloody vengeance upon the white man. But the end was not far off. General Davis reached the Lava Beds on the 2d of May, 1873. He found the troops much depressed; the loss of beloved comrades, the cheerless winter camps, and repeated failures against a foe so small in numbers had impaired their zeal and confidence. A few days were necessary to reorganize the command and cheer the drooping spirits of the men, and General Davis took the opportunity to send two friendly squaws of the Modoc tribe into the Lava Beds. They returned after two days, exhausted from fatigue, and reported that the Indians had gone away quite recently.

Vigorous pursuit was ordered. Too much exhausted to escape by flight, the

desperate and sagacious foe turned, surprised, and attacked the camp of the
troops. But the struggle had now become more than ever unequal. They
were easily repulsed, and retreated in the
direction of the Lava Beds, hotly contest-
ing every foot of the way with the pursuing troops, until the whole band was
again lodged in the rocky fastnesses. The
pursuit was active and close, while a body
of troops advanced rapidly from the opposite direction. The Indians, thus threatened with attacks from two sides, were
sandwiched but not surrounded. Their
position was now desperate, and the indomitable chief resorted to desperate measures to keep his weary warriors up to
their work. But insubordination and dis-
sensions sprang up, and the band separated into two parties, bitter enemies, and
both left the Lava Beds. One band, vigor-
ously pursued by the troops, surrendered,
coming into camp on the 22d of May and
laying down their arms. They were accompanied by their old men, women, and

children, in all about one hundred and
fifty. But Captain Jack and his principal
followers were still at large. The cavalry
force sought them in all directions. At
last the betrayer was betrayed. One of
the Modoc captives, who had been in the
confidence of Captain Jack, offered to lead
the troops to his hiding-place. After some
hesitation the offer was accepted. Jack's
camp was reached and the Modoc captive
entered it. A stormy interview with the
angry chief ensued. Jack denounced the
deserters in severe terms for leaving him,
and declared that he would die with his
gun in his hand. On the 29th of May the
troops were pushed rapidly forward after
the desperate fugitive. They were now in
excellent spirits. The Lava Beds were at
last behind them, and the flying enemy
was in a comparatively open country. The
day of retribution was at hand. The pursuit was kept up with vigor, and Jack and
the remnant of his band were discovered
on Willow Creek, near its crossing with
the old emigrant road. They scattered

and fled and were picked up in detail. Finally, on the 3d of June, Jack was captured with two or three other warriors. When surrounded and taken prisoner he merely said: "My legs have given out," and relapsed into the stoical indifference characteristic of his race.

Thus ended another act in this great drama. By the 5th of June the whole band, with a few unimportant exceptions, had been captured and conveyed to the camp at Tule Lake. The iron hand of justice was now extended to clutch the malefactors. The commander of the troops designed to execute some eight or ten of the leaders on the spot. Having made known, however, the fact of their capture to the authorities at Washington, he received orders to hold them under guard until further instructions were given as to the disposition to be made of them. The purpose to try them by a military commission gave rise to several questions which were quite fully weighed by the authorities as well as discussed in the papers of the day,

Peace men were earnest and active on the side of mercy to the criminals. The Attorney-General of the United States decided that a military commission might legally take cognizance of the case. Accordingly, that tribunal was constituted by General Davis's order, and directed to meet at Fort Klamath, Oregon, on the 1st of July, 1873, "for the trial of the Modoc chief known as Captain Jack, and such other Indian captives as may properly be brought before it."

This proceeding threw the mantle of formality around the condemnation of the doomed men and added to the solemnity of the occasion. Their guilt was undoubted, and their crime black and premeditated; but yet it was a sickening sight to see those six vanquished savages—Captain Jack, Schonchin, Black Jim, Boston Charley, Barncho, and Sloluck—arraigned for ceremonious trial before the cultivated, uniformed victors against whom they had waged such desperate and unequal war. Manacled, haggard, and forlorn, they filed

into the court-room and faced the five
officers in whose hands their fate rested. With one exception, none of them
understood the English language, and all
had but a faint conception of the meaning of the ceremonies which they wit-
nessed in the organization of the commission. They were asked through the
interpreter if they objected to any of the
members, and each distinctly answered,
"*No*." When asked if they desired to
introduce counsel, they severally replied
in the negative, adding that *they had been
unable to procure any*. The trial proceeded. They were duly arraigned on the
charges, 1st, "Murder, in violation of the
laws of war"; and, 2d, "Assault with in-
tent to kill, in violation of the laws of
war." Riddle, Tobe, Dyar, and Meacham
were the witnesses for the prosecution.
They told the story of the assassination,
without cross-examination by the accused.
Tobe related the events with great accuracy. Her own remarkable behavior was
mentioned with perfect simplicity. Slo-

luck hit her across the back with his gun and knocked her down. "Then," said she, "he was going to strike me again. He was talking to me, and trying to get the horse. Captain Jack and another Indian told him to let me alone: Black Jim, there, and Jack." Then, according to the evidence, from the midst of the terrible slaughter which she had foreseen but could not avert, with her murdered friends and fleeing husband in sight, and with the spiteful bullets whistling about her ears, this undaunted woman trudged deliberately back to camp, *leading her slow paced horse.*

The trial now produced the rare spectacle of Indian state's evidence. Shacknasty Jim, Hooker Jim, Steamboat Frank, and Bogus Charley, all guilty, took the stand against their brethren and companions in crime, and testified to the conspiracy and the details of the tragedy. The oath administered to these witnesses (?), and the warning against the sin of lying and the crime of perjury given them

by the Judge-Advocate, appeared like solemn mockery. They testified to the conspiracy, confessed their respective parts in
it, and stated that they had turned against
Captain Jack, the leader.

The prisoners declined to question them.

The testimony for the defence was the
most characteristic feature of this extraordinary trial. The witnesses were
Indians—Scar-faced Charley, Dave, and
One-eyed Mose. No effort was made to
controvert what the prosecution had established. The only purpose of the accused seemed to be to implicate their
enemies, the Klamaths. Captain Jack's
examination of his witnesses was very
simple, and was alike for all of them.
Scar-faced Charley was the first one
called. Cautioned against perjury under
the white man's law, he took the white
man's oath.

Question by Captain Jack.—"Tell about
Link-River Jack coming and giving us
powder and stuff."

Answer.—"The first time was down

here at Ellen's, at the east end of the
Lava Beds. We were attacked there by
the soldiers, and there were some Klamath Lake Indians along with the soldiers
there, and they told us not to shoot at
them, but to shoot at the soldiers—the
Klamaths did. We killed one soldier
down close to Louis Lands, at the east
end of the Lava Beds. That was directly
after the fight at Lost River. The Klamath Lake Indians told me that they did
not expect to be friends to the soldiers all
the time ; that they would be our friends
after a while. After that they came with
the soldiers to our stronghold in the Lava
Beds and fought us. In the fight there
were ten of them came to us, and they
gave us most of the ammunition we had.
One in particular, Link-River Jack, gave
us ammunition and guns. One-eye Link-
River then gave his powder-horn full of
powder to Indian George, a Modoc ; he
poured it all out and gave it all to him
that was in his horn. The day before the
fight of January 17, Little John told me

to fight hard the next day, and whip the soldiers and kill all we could. The way we got most of our ammunition after the fight of 17th of January was, we went round and picked up the cartridges, and the Klamath Lakes gave us some, and we opened the cartridges and got at the powder, and then made bullets of the lead that was in them. We had plenty of caps. The Klamath Lakes told us not to shoot them, that they were our friends; and I drew my pistol out and told them that they were the cause of the fight, that they had urged it on; and they said, No, that they were always our friends. We had a long talk. I told them then to leave all the ammunition that they had and could get; to pile it under a rock there where we were, and I could get it. I told them: 'You say you are our friends, and I want to see whether you are or not.' I went the next day, and found the ammunition there; there was a flour-sack half-full. I got one hundred rounds of ammunition myself that they left there. I then asked the Klamaths if they were telling the truth, and they said they were; that Allen David had told them to tell me that they would not fight us; that when they went there they went to shoot up, to make the soldiers believe they were our enemies, but they were our friends. That is all I know."

Captain Jack said he had no other questions to ask this witness. The testimony of his other witnesses was the same substantially as the foregoing extract. Such was the pitiable effort made by these unaided and unlettered malefactors when on trial for their lives.

Captain Jack and Schonchin spoke in their own defence. Their remarks were in keeping with the testimony they introduced. Captain Jack said: "I hardly know how to talk here. I don't know how white people talk in such a place as this; but I will do the best I can. I will talk about Judge Roseborough first. He always told me to be a good man. Roseborough never gave me any advice but good advice. He told me to be a good man and do the right thing by my fellow-men. I considered myself as a white man. I took passes from good white men who gave me good advice. I knew all the people that were living about the country, and they all knew that I was an honest man. You men here don't know what I have been heretofore. I never accused any white man of being mean and bad. No white man can say that I ever objected to their coming to live in my country. I would like to see the man who ever knew me to do anything wrong heretofore. Nobody ever called me mean except the Klamath Indians. I would like to see the man who started this fuss and caused me to be in the trouble I am in now.

"They scared me when they came to where I was living on Lost River and started this fight. I cannot understand why they were mad with me. I have always told the white man to come and settle in my country. I have never received anything from anybody only what I

bought and paid for myself. Riddle
knows that I have always lived like a
man, and have never gone begging. He
has always given me good advice and told
me to live like a white man, and I have always tried to do it, and did do it until the
war started. It scared me when Major
Jackson came and got there just at daylight, and made me jump out of my bed
without a shirt or anything else on. I did
not know what it meant, his coming at
that time of day. When Major Jackson
and his men came up to my camp they
surrounded it, and I hollered to Major
Jackson for them not to shoot, that I
would talk. I told Bogus Charley to go
and talk until I could get my clothes on.
He went and told them that he wanted to
talk, that he didn't want them to shoot.
Then they all got down off their horses,
and I thought then we were going to have
a talk, and I went into another tent. I
thought then why were they mad at me?
What had they found out about me, that
they came here to fight me? I went into

my tent then, and I sat down, and they commenced shooting. My people were not all there. There were but a few of us there. Major Jackson shot my men while they were standing around. They shot some of my women, and they shot my men." He extended his remarks in the same strain, and accused Hooker Jim and others who had appeared against him.

The Judge-Advocate made a few remarks to bring out the fact that Major Jackson acted only in compliance with the orders he had received from his superior officer, made at the request of the Indian Department, to have the Modocs returned to the Klamath Reservation.

The Indians were conducted back to their prison, and the Commission, after deliberation for a brief period, found each and every one of the accused guilty of both charges, and sentenced them to be hanged by the neck until dead.

The proceedings were approved by General Davis and transmitted for the orders of the President of the United States, by

whom they were approved, and on the 23d
of August the War Department order was
made for the execution at Fort Klamath,
Oregon, on Friday, October 3, 1873.

The scaffold was erected, and at the
time and place designated the doomed
savages were brought from their prison
under a strong guard; their manacles
were removed, but their arms were tightly
pinioned with cords, and, placed in a
wagon, they were hauled, in the centre of
an ample guard, to the spot from which
they were to take their departure for another world. Wretched and miserable in
appearance, they trod the scaffold with
apparent indifference, having evidently
resolved to die as bravely as they had
lived. Seated on the platform of the scaffold, with their feet on the drop, they lis-
tened to the reading of the sentence. An
order commuting the sentences of Barncho
and Sloluck to imprisonment for life was
then read, and these two shackled malefactors were returned to their dungeons.

A prayer was offered by the chaplain,

the nooses placed about the necks of the culprits, and the black caps drawn over their heads. As the drop fell with a heavy "thud," a half-smothered cry of horror went up from the crowd of over five hundred Klamath Indians who wit- nessed the awful spectacle. Wails of bit- ter anguish also arose from the stockade, from which the wives and children of the poor creatures viewed the shocking scene. They were gone at last, and could no more be forced back to the hated Klamath Re- servation.

The remaining members of the ill-fated band were soon sent to the Indian Terri- tory, where a small area was allotted to them a few miles from Baxter Springs, Kansas. There they still remain. They have built log-houses, enclosed fields, and cultivate the soil in severalty. But dis- ease and death have made sad havoc among them. More than one hundred and fifty arrived in 1873, but they now do not number a hundred. When asked of their welfare, they answer they are sick,

that many die, and, pointing to the grave-
yard, say sadly that too many lie there.
They marry, the children attend school,
and the band is industrious. They slowly
adopt some of the ways of civilization.
Captain Jack's widow has consoled herself
with another husband, but, although marriage and remarriage goes on, they do not
increase in numbers, the deaths exceeding
the births.

As a tribe the Modocs have ceased to
exist. Suffering from wrongs that entitled
them to sympathy and assistance, they
took the law into their own hands, and
worked savage vengeance, not upon the
men who had injured them, but on those
who were striving to save and provide for
them. In blind fury they treacherously
entrapped and murdered their two best
friends. For this hideous crime four of
their principal men have paid in full on
the scaffold, two are doomed to rot for life
in Alcatraz prison, and the remainder, in
banishment, are fast fading away by disease and despair.